You Can Only Achieve
What Is Possible

A SELF-HELP
'ANTIDOTE' TO OUR
SELF-HELP CULTURE

First published by O Books, 2008
O Books is an imprint of John Hunt Publishing Ltd., The Bothy, Deershot Lodge, Park Lane, Ropley,
Hants, SO24 0BE, UK
office1@o-books.net
www.o-books.net

Distribution in:	South Africa
	Alternative Books
UK and Europe	altbook@peterhyde.co.za
Orca Book Services	Tel: 021 555 4027 Fax: 021 447 1430
orders@orcabookservices.co.uk	
Tel: 01202 665432 Fax: 01202 666219	Text copyright Dawn Mellowship 2008
Int. code (44)	
	ISBN: 978 1 84694 109 2
USA and Canada	
NBN	All rights reserved. Except for brief quotations
custserv@nbnbooks.com	in critical articles or reviews, no part of this
Tel: 1 800 462 6420 Fax: 1 800 338 4550	book may be reproduced in any manner without
	prior written permission from the publishers.
Australia and New Zealand	
Brumby Books	The rights of Dawn Mellowship as author have
sales@brumbybooks.com.au	been asserted in accordance with the
Tel: 61 3 9761 5535 Fax: 61 3 9761 7095	Copyright, Designs and Patents Act 1988.
Far East (offices in Singapore, Thailand,	
Hong Kong, Taiwan)	
Pansing Distribution Pte Ltd	
kemal@pansing.com	A CIP catalogue record for this book is available
Tel: 65 6319 9939 Fax: 65 6462 5761	from the British Library.

Printed by Chris Fowler International
www.chrisfowler.com

O Books operates a distinctive and ethical publishing philosophy in
all areas of its business, from its global network of authors to
production and worldwide distribution.
This book is produced on FSC certified stock, within ISO14001
standards. The printer plants sufficient trees each year through
the Woodland Trust to absorb the level of emitted carbon in
its production.

You Can Only Achieve
What Is Possible

A SELF-HELP
'ANTIDOTE' TO OUR
SELF-HELP CULTURE

Dawn Mellowship

BOOKS

Winchester, UK
Washington, USA

This book is dedicated to God, Jesus Christ, Andrew Chrysostomou and to all the souls who will one day be enlightened.

The only real valuable thing is intuition.

Albert Einstein

We follow the ways of wolves, the habits of tigers: or, rather we are worse than they. To them nature has assigned that they should be thus fed, while God has honoured us with rational speech and a sense of equity. And yet we are become worse than the wild beast.

John Chrysostom, C. 345-407, Homily, LXIX, Chapter 4

I like your Christ, I do not like your Christians. Your Christians are so unlike your Christ.

Mahatma Gandhi

Everyone thinks of changing the world, but no one thinks of changing himself.

Leo Tolstoy

The saviour answered...and said, "If you want to be perfect, you will keep these teachings. If not, you deserve to be called ignorant. For a wise person cannot associate with a fool. The wise person is perfect in all wisdom, but to the fool, good and evil are one and the same. For the wise person will be nourished by the truth...Some people have wings but run after what they can see, what is far from the truth."

The Book of Thomas

Jesus said, "If you bring forth what is within you, what you bring forth will save you. If you do not bring forth what is within you, what you do not bring forth will destroy you."

The Gospel of Thomas

Contents

Introduction

The self-improvement industry is a multi-billion dollar one. In 2004, Amazon had a 38% increase in sales of self-help books. So many people are clamouring for ways to improve their health, their lives and their spiritual well-being. More of us are happy to take our health into our own hands. For many people, the niggling feeling that something is missing in their lives will not abate. There is a wealth of literature for us to choose from. If you walk into your local bookstore you will probably find a number of shelves stacked with self-help and spiritual books. Some of these books will have glowing, celebrity endorsements,

For anything you could ever possibly want to achieve, there is probably a self-help book, or expert that would be happy to offer you some advice. Whether you are looking for money, motivation, confidence, spiritual fulfilment or the attainment of your goals, there is something somewhere that promises to give you the answers you have been looking for.

Whilst it is fantastic that individuals are taking such an interest in improving their lives, the self-help genre is also a minefield, with a mixed bag of information. Some of it is fantastic, some of it is good, some of it is passable and some of it is sheer twaddle. Although it is highly commendable that many human beings are seeking answers, quite a significant proportion of individuals are hankering after easy answers; the answers that require the least amount of effort. By the same token there are some, *some* I might add, not *all*, self-help experts, who readily proffer easy answers.

The easy answers necessitate minimal action on your part, like, for example, the concept that, all you have to do is submit your wish list to the Universe and your desires will be fulfilled. The Universe is not a local take-away or a high class hooker offering optional added extras. It is not here to serve our whims. If we want something, we have to work for it and be thoroughly prepared to accept the consequences. This is just a paradigm, of what you can find out there. I could give many more, but I will not, or that will spoil the rest of this book.

So, everyone is left in a situation where they have to separate the good, from the bad, from the downright ugly. The ugly can appear to be incredibly good because it offers what you want to hear. The good can seem ugly because it questions your belief system and proposes alterations in your lifestyle that require real effort. We are left in a quandary over what option we should choose. I posit that we should choose our intuition. It sounds so glaringly obvious. It is not rocket science, there is no special code required. We just need to be fully aware of and take heed of our intuitive guidance. Our intuition is never mistaken and if we listen to it intently, we can take what we require from the self-help literature and experts that we admire and then disband the rest.

With this all in mind and in frustration at what I have witnessed and read, I decided to write some self-help books of my own. This is not without irony. In this particular piece of work I avidly question some of the more popular self-help theories, concepts, beliefs, or whatever you deem fit to call them. I have provided alternatives, well, you may call them theories, or beliefs. I would declare them to be my intuition.

Each chapter begins with, what I term, 'A Tall Tale,' or in other terms, a big fat fib. These stories are all just that, entirely fictitious, not based on any real people, or events and so on. They are simply there to illustrate my point. I did try to make some of them mildly entertaining, but for the most part, as in life, I only amuse myself. They are not intended to be hysterically funny, this is in truth, a serious piece of work and quite a number of them are pretty sombre. However to cheer you up, the little fictions are accompanied by slightly more amusing cartoons. If they cause offence to anyone, I do not apologise. If we take offence too easily, we need to re-evaluate our priorities in life.

With your appetite whetted by the Tall Tales you will reach sections entitled, 'Seriously Though.' Obviously, these are naturally intended to broach serious and poignant issues. However, sometimes I could not resist being a *tad* sarcastic. I do not believe this diminishes the value of the points I am making, rather it heightens them, because it does not *all* have to be entirely bleak. It is fine to laugh at ourselves and at each other. Self-help can be fun, spiritual development can be an absolute blast and you do not have to exude love and light to everyone you meet. Instead, you get to be your real self and brutally honest with it.

I do tend to state my case with conviction because I know what I know, but whether you choose to believe it or not, is up to you. I am not a preacher, although sometimes I may come across as slightly preachy and what you believe is, of course, entirely your own choice. It is never enough for us to hear the words; we have to experience the true significance of those words for ourselves. Take away with you, what you intuitively feel you need from this book. Questioning is vital, question away, it helps us all to learn.

I do keep labouring the point about trusting in your intuition, throughout the book, in the hope that my labour and toil will get the cogs of your intuition ticking over nicely. Without an intuitive connection we become a ticking time bomb waiting to explode and real happiness can never come to pass, until we re-kindle the flame we have extinguished. If I seem dogmatic, that is because, I suppose, in some ways, I am. I do not claim to know all truths. I am not God, but I do know some truths and these I have shared.

You too, know many truths, many more than you even dare to realise. Within you are all the answers you could ever possibly need for your path in this life and beyond, you just need to access those answers. Hopefully, this book will go some way towards helping you unleash the true extent of your own inner wisdom. The hard work that will take you there is all down to you.

At the end of each chapter there are techniques that you can use to foster your own intuition. They will not work overnight miracles, life will not suddenly become a walk in the park and they do not promise to accommodate all your worldly desires. What do they do? The techniques will help you, if practised often, with strong intention and purpose, to find the real you, or more precisely, in more spiritual terms, your soul. Effort is definitely required, as are good thoughts and good actions. You may not get everything you desire, but you can get everything you need. With our good friend, time, you will come to desire what you need.

If you think the methods are nonsense, you can do two things: do them anyway and see what happens, or do not bother to do them at all and see what happens. This is the exquisite beauty of choice. It is what separates us from our animal friends. Humans do not, as it is commonly believed, behave in a bestial way, because animals are governed by the instinct sanctioned to them. Humans instead, are frequently beyond the beast, because for all their choices, their barbarity knows no bounds. We would all do well to use our choices wisely. Some people do, but not as often as they should.

What gives me *any* authority to presume? I wield no authority over you. None of us really possess authority, not in the way we believe we do. Power is an illusion, because the earth is not ours and it can be snatched away from us in a mere moment. I relinquish my power to God, or if that term troubles you, the Universe.

I do believe in God, but not in the 'religious' sense that has become so customary. Rather I perceive God as a creative, intelligent, loving, energy. In reality, God is so much more than my words, or any words, could ever do justice to. However, bound by the poverty of language, I will keep the description short and sweet. The reason I am drawing your attention to this, is that I use the term God fairly liberally in the book and, more frequently, so as not to evoke negative stereo-typing, I use the term, the Universe. Sometimes I also say, Divine.

If you believe in God, then you will be completely at ease with the term. If you believe in something, but prefer not to bestow the label God, name it as you see fit. A tag does not alter what God is. If you do not believe in God, that is OK. I am sure you can still identify with the term intuition, as a form of inner wisdom or innate instinct. Although, for what it is worth, I do not believe that anyone can really gaze up at the stars, witness the intricate and complex elegance of the Universe and not, deep down, feel the existence of a higher force at work.

Now, about me, I am a Reiki teacher and practitioner. Reiki, as I practise it, is a Japanese energy healing system, discovered in the early 1900s. It is often used in a very flaky and passive way, but I like to use it in an active and practical way. Reiki transformed my life. I found my purpose in life and regained an intuitive connection that I had lost, or more aptly, squandered, in the past. I irresponsibly pursued my physical desires to the absolute detriment of my own health, well-being, self-development and, of course, my spirituality. Although, all was not lost, with hard work, dedication, right living and right thinking, I re-captured my lost forlorn soul. Anyone can re-capture their soul or self, if they take the right course of action. As Jesus Christ said, according to the Book of Thomas, "For whoever does not know self does not know anything, but whoever knows self already, has acquired knowledge about the depths of the Universe." [1]

I learned from my lessons and I continue to learn. I accept that in Universal knowledge terms, I am probably a toddler and perhaps one day, I will grow up to be an adult. We are all so much smaller than we dare to realise and if we can acknowledge this, we can come to truly evolve and grow. Only then, can we harvest adults in this melancholy world.

On that note, I will leave you to peruse the rest of this book in peace and quiet. I hope that you will, at least, find it engaging. I sincerely hope that it will achieve so much more.

The secret has at last been unleashed, it is called your intuition, it was never really a secret, but the term sounded so captivating and mysterious. The truth is not an enigma. It is blindingly obvious to those who see beyond what their eyes can see. Without further ado, I present to you, You Can Only Achieve What Is Possible.

---

[1] The Book of Thomas; The Secret Teachings Of Jesus: Four Gnostic Gospels, 1:6, p41, Translated by Marvin W. Meyer, First Vintage Books, 1984.

"The words printed here are concepts. You must go through the experiences."

Saint Augustine

Feel The Fear And Run Away...

...because rational fear protects you

A Tall Tale

I read a book that told me that I should face my fears head on and that I should not be afraid. I wanted to do something brave and bold that would snap me out of my comfort zone. I thought of one of my worst fears, mountain climbing and just one week later I made a bold, or perhaps stupid decision, to book myself onto a mountain trekking adventure.

The day came to embark upon my journey. I headed out to the mountains and I could hardly stop shaking as the tour guide spelled out the day's itinerary. Why on earth had I decided to do this? I felt it was the only way to overcome my fear of mountain climbing.

I will never forget the moment when I hovered at the base of a mountain. I was simultaneously terrified and filled with awe, at this monolithic, towering structure. I looked up at the towering peak. I heard the wind growling. "Growling?" I thought, "The wind doesn't growl." Suddenly, I felt this hot breath on the back of my neck and a shiver travelled through my spine. Dare I look behind me? Not a chance, I rocketed up that mountain with the tour guide shouting all the way for me to hurry.

The bear took a swipe at me and there was absolutely no way I was staying behind to discover what would happen next. Luckily, the bear lost interest after pacing at the base of the mountain for a few minutes, relieved itself and wandered off. I felt lucky to have escaped relatively unscathed.

Mountains; I hate them. I live in a big city, why do I need to climb mountains? My advice; feel the fear and run away!

Some Common Fears...

- ❑ Fear of not being good enough
- ❑ Fear of failure
- ❑ Fear of getting emotionally hurt
- ❑ Fear of taking responsibility
- ❑ Fear of being judged by others

Some Unusual Fears...

- ❑ Acarophobia – the fear of itching
- ❑ Amensiophobia – the fear of amnesia
- ❑ Androphobia – the fear of women
- ❑ Autophobia – the fear of yourself
- ❑ Barophobia – the fear of gravity

Seriously Though...

Fear has an important part to play in our lives. Rational fear protects us when we are in treacherous situations. I'd like to keep some of my fears thanks, like the one that prevents me from sauntering down a dark alleyway at night alone, or the fear that prevents me from placing my hand on the red hot cooker hob. Having no fears is all well and good if the world were a perfect place inhabited by perfect people, but alas this is not the case. The world is a dangerous and scary place and fear helps us to survive. That is not an irrational fear, but a fact of life.

Thirty years ago, some people would leave their front doors ajar and let their neighbours wander in and out of their houses at will. There are probably some areas where people are still able to safely do this, but in many areas it is far too risky. People generally refrain from leaving their front doors open because of a rational fear of the consequences, such as an opportunistic burglar popping in to steal all their worldly goods. Some individuals have no fear of anything and they will think nothing of murdering someone for sport, or as we have seen in the United States and United Kingdom, beating up or burning a homeless person for sheer kicks, with no fear of the repercussions. **No fear is no good.**

If you have no fear at all, you can open yourself up to hazardous situations, or if someone is completely fearless of the consequences and lacks an intuitive connection, they can perform unsavoury actions that are detrimental to the lives of themselves and potentially to others. When you reprimand a child for incorrect behaviour, they need to have some level of fear; otherwise they will never learn the consequences of bad actions. Our schools are teeming with youths who know their

human rights, but lack basic discipline and a fear of anyone
or anything. Some of these young people behave recklessly
and in certain cases, this is partly attributable to their lack of
discipline, upbringing and lack of fear. The truth is we need
fear. It sustains as well as destroys us.

The key is to strike a balance in assessing whether our
fears are rational or irrational fears. Perhaps, you are longing
to undertake a certain career but are too afraid to follow your
dreams. You need to ascertain whether this fear is because
your dream is not within your remit in relation to your path
on this earth, or whether this fear is completely unfounded.
The best way to achieve this is by trusting your intuition.

"So, what exactly *is* intuition?" I hear you say. We all
have souls that inhabit and animate our human bodies. These
souls are our connection to the Universe or God, if you like.
Our souls are pure high frequency energy. I will explain all of
these concepts more thoroughly throughout the book, but to
get you started, our souls communicate with our physical and
emotional bodies through our intuition. In others words, our
intuition is the voice of our souls.

Our spiritual bodies or if you prefer, our souls, are
the highest frequency, purest energies of all our bodies. They
are closest to the Divine or the Divine spark within us. By
being close to the Divine, our souls possess the greatest level
of knowledge and awareness of all our bodies; hence we
should follow our intuition.

Depending on how close our souls are to the Divine,
or God, we have either more or less knowledge of ourselves
and the external Universe. Some of us are more connected to
our intuition and spiritual bodies than others, which I will
further elaborate on later in this chapter. The strength of our
connection to our souls determines our level of intuition and

how strong the connection is, depends on how we have lived our lives and how our lives have affected us.

The main thing to remember is that if you trust your intuition implicitly, you will never ever go wrong in life. The knowledge imparted to us through our intuition, is way above and beyond that of both our physical and our emotional bodies. The latter two, only function effectively if dominated by our souls.

If you do not know how to trust your intuition, you need to learn fast. That little niggling, seldom acknowledged, voice in the back of your head that says, "I told you not to do that", or "I told you he or she was bad news", or "I told you not to go there," *that* is the voice you need to be listening to. That voice that tells you, "You cannot possibly be the next great singing sensation, because you lack the singing talent," or that, "You cannot be an Olympic athlete, because you are useless at running." The voice that whispers, "You should get the later train today, because the early one is not coming." The voice of your intuition, the voice that desperately tries to communicate to you that you are running through life in such a manic way because you are utterly lost for answers.

There are some techniques at the end of this chapter that will give you a firm helping hand, but the rest of the hard work, is up to you.

Your intuition is your greatest guide and should be your best friend for life. Get to know the difference between your intuition, physical desires and emotional desires. Your physical body and emotions should be heading in the same direction as your intuition. If they are veering off in disparate directions, you will never be truly happy, because you will find yourself being pulled three ways. If you can learn how to wholeheartedly trust your intuition, you will not even need to read the rest of this book.

If you are struggling to hear your intuitive voice, to begin with, then you have to think, is this what I need or just what I want? Are my fears founded or unfounded, rational or irrational? Am I terrified of asking my manager for a pay rise, because he will react badly, or am I afraid of asking for what I deserve? Am I petrified of re-locating to distant shores, because I have a purpose for being where I am now, or am I just afraid of any change at all? Am I afraid of entering adult education because it is not the right place for me, or am I afraid of the studying and my own insecurities? Ask yourself why you have this fear, before you jump on the bandwagon of banishing that fear.

Remember, fear in itself is not a bad thing. Our earth notions of what is good and bad are not quite the same on a universal scale. You need to have *some* fear. It helps you to question your motives; whether they are through instinct and intuition, pursuit of physical wants and desires, emotional crutches, or whatever. Your fears also help you to question the motives of others. Does that individual at work make you feel uncomfortable, because your intuition is telling you to beware, or do they make you feel uncomfortable because they make you question your own life? Some fear keeps you in your allotted place in the Universe, following your path. Some fear prevents anarchy. Too much fear can stall your personal and spiritual development. Strike a balance. Work out if your fears are rational or irrational, intuitive or self-constructed.

A **rational fear** has a purpose for your path on earth and it protects you from dangerous situations. Rational fear is your intuition conversing with you via your physical body and your emotions. Your soul does not feel fear, but being trapped inside your body, the only way it can keep you on the right track is by provoking a physical or emotional response. One of the messages these bodies understand in relation to that provocation is fear. Once you become enlightened, your soul no longer needs to converse through emotions, because you automatically know what to do, you only listen to your intuition. In the absence of absolute intuition, your soul relies on all your other faculties.

An **irrational fear** is your emotional and physical bodies communicating with you, without input from your intuition or soul. Irrational fears are often created from your upbringing, your social conditioning and your state of mind. The less intuitive you are, the more likely you will be to have many irrational rather than rational fears. In the absence of intuition, we tread a very unsteady path that relies heavily on our physical and emotional bodies. These two bodies have a limited foundation of knowledge, based on their experiences of life from a physical perspective.

The distinct lack of a connection to our souls disables us from feeling Divine love and this lacking terrifies us, so we search for a solution in all the wrong places. Some irrational fears, like the fear of consuming fruit, are the consequence of emotional traumas we have experienced throughout our lives. It is important to distinguish between the two types of fear, before relegating fear to the docks.

Rational Fear
Your intuition telling you to do something to protect you and the message your emotional and physical bodies understand in relation to that is fear.

Irrational Fear
Fears deriving from your physical or emotional bodies without any input from your intuition. The lack of an intuitive connection or a weak connection causes irrational fears, as does our conditioning.

Some Rational Fears

☑ Fear of going out at night alone in an area with a high crime rate.

☑ Fear of letting your eight year old child walk to school on his or her own.

☑ Fear of getting rejected on a TV singing talent contest because you know you can't sing.

☑ Fear of asking for a pay rise because you know your boss is in the process of firing employees.

☑ Fear of leaving your baby in their buggy outside a supermarket while you go in and shop.

☑ Fear of entering a relationship with a violent alcoholic.

☑ Fear of breaking the law because of the necessary consequences.

☑ Fear of drinking too much alcohol in case you end up having unprotected sex with a stranger.

☑ Fear of walking on hot coals in case you get your feet burnt.

☑ Fear of not brushing your teeth at least twice a day in case they decay.

☑ Fear of eating bread because you are allergic to wheat.

☑ Fear of re-locating because your intuition is telling you it is not the right thing to do.

☑ Fear of having children because you are not in a happy or stable environment to support them.

☑ Fear of cancer because several family members have had it.

Some Irrational Fears

☒ Fear of trusting your intuition because it will change the course of your life.

☒ Fear of taking responsibility for yourself.

☒ Fear of letting go of the past.

☒ Fear of loving yourself unconditionally.

☒ Fear of attaining real happiness.

☒ Fear of facing the reality of your life and the truth.

☒ Fear of being loved unconditionally.

☒ Fear of letting the will of the Universe guide your life, rather than trying to control everything.

☒ Fear of breaking bad habits.

☒ Fear of putting yourself first, rather than others.

☒ Fear of living a healthier lifestyle because it might alienate you socially.

☒ Fear of distancing yourself from negative people, for the same reason as above.

☒ Fear of being alone.

☒ Fear of being judged by others.

☒ Fear of expressing yourself.

☒ Fear of God.

☒ Fear of death.

What Do I Do?

Once you have firmly established through intuition which of your fears are rational and irrational, you are going to have to decide precisely what to do about them. For some fears you will not need to do anything. If you have a fear of bungee jumping, then quite simply, do not go out and do a bungee jump. There is no rule book anywhere that says your life will be less rich, if you do not undertake dare devil activities. If you *need* to jump out of a plane or off a bridge to get a thrill out of life, there must be something lacking somewhere else. There is no point in us getting all worked up about activities that we need never undertake.

I used to be somewhat scared of heights, not overly so, but the prospect of falling out of the sky is never a joyful one. Some well-known self-help experts believe the only way to overcome a fear is to face it head on. I went to Australia when I was nineteen and decided to do a bungee jump, not because I was facing my fears. I was young and out to have a good time. I did the bungee jump. It was pretty scary, I sort of enjoyed it, in a fleeting way, but it was over in seconds. Did the experience enrich my life? No. Did it make me any less scared of heights? No. Did it change me as a person? Not a bit.

I do not buy all the self-help bumph that claims that facing these sorts of fears transforms our lives for the better. If someone wants to go and walk on hot coals to prove that they can do it, that is fine, but it will not heal their emotional traumas, or transform them into a more spiritually evolved or improved human being. Fundamentally, I believe that the only way we can radically transform our lives for the better, is by trusting in and following our intuition, by our right living, our right thinking and our right actions. Walking on very hot coals, whooping and saying, "yeah man I can do it!" will not connect us with our souls. Such activities are short term fixes, well not even that. They are gimmicks.

Raising the frequencies of our bodies and emotions, to that of our souls, is the path to enlightenment. There are numerous ways to achieve this wonderful state of being and the aforementioned activities do not form any of them.

It is not always easy for people to trust in and follow their intuition, because they amass various emotional traumas throughout their lives that form blockages to their personal development. To change their lives, all these traumas need to be addressed.

In my opinion, our emotional traumas form negative energies within our physical and emotional bodies and these energies stall our progress in life as they accumulate and grow over the years. Unless these negative energies are eliminated, we can never truly move on, regardless of how much we talk about an issue or try to convince ourselves that we have dealt with it.

The most effective way I have personally found to eradicate these blockages is Reiki, a Japanese energy healing system. Anyone can take a Reiki course and become a healer. Learning Reiki is a bit like meditating on a mountain top for thirty years, without the meditation...or being on a mountain top. Through a process called attunements, which connect you to Universal energy and your intuition and by constant self-healing on a daily basis, you can achieve in weeks, what many people on a spiritual or self-help quest do not achieve in an entire lifetime.

There are various alternative ways to connect to your intuitive voice, such as: Qi-Gong, meditation, prayer, spiritual and other forms of healing, but they can take a lot longer.

It is not enough to walk on some hot coals, or tread a tightrope, which gives us an artificial and fleeting confidence. We need the real confidence that comes from following our true paths on earth and trusting our inner guidance. When we can achieve this, we do not feel the need to jump off bridges, or climb mountains, or walk tight-ropes, because we know that in real terms it is meaningless. When we are enlightened, our satisfaction comes from the unconditional love we feel from our Divine connection and no feeling on earth can top that.

In essence, I have no issue with people doing bungee jumps, sky-diving, snowboarding, mountain climbing and so on, if that is what they want to do and they enjoy it. I do, however, have a problem with people claiming that it is a way to deal with their fears and emotional traumas.

I could easily have trod the fiery embers at nineteen. I might even have enjoyed it and felt a momentary confidence boost, but ultimately, it would not have changed my life. It would not have persuaded me to take more responsibility for my actions, or boosted my self-esteem. The only thing that enabled me to achieve that was self-healing every single day through Reiki. This helped me to become my true higher self and have faith in my intuition. Each of us needs to find our own way of attaining this state.

However you choose to go about doing it, knowing and becoming your true self, without anything holding you back is the *only* way to really understand and overcome your fears in life. The rest is peripheral.

Rational Fears

Having fears does not mean that you have to be controlled by them. You **can** do something about them, if something needs to be done. The fact that you are aware of those fears means that you are aware of the consequences and you can introduce specific changes in your life to prevent those fears becoming an unpleasant reality. Rather than thinking, "oh my goodness I have this awful fear," be glad that you are aware of it, because that fear is helping you to perceive the potential consequences. That fear can rouse you into necessary action to avoid those consequences becoming a reality. This is why your intuition gives you a nudge and says, "Hey we should do something about this."

You will notice that in the rational fears list on page eight, there are both some glaringly obvious fears that require little thought and some not quite so obvious fears that need much more consideration. As I discussed above, certain fears require no action at all, like walking a tight-rope, climbing a tree, jumping off a bridge, treading hot coals etc. Some fears require very little action. Fear of going out late at night alone, can be resolved by simply not going out late at night alone. Fear of letting your eight year child walk to school alone can be resolved fairly easily, by finding a way to personally escort them to school everyday. Alternatively, perhaps you could talk to another parent in your locality who takes their child to the same school and ask them if they would be happy to take your child to school as well.

If your fear is related to a dream of yours, then you need to understand why you have that fear. Is it an intuitive fear or an irrational fear? I mentioned the television singing contest in the rational fears list as a joke, but it demonstrates my point very well. We have all seen well known television contests, where contestants are astonished to hear from the judges that they have no talent in that field whatsoever. The contestants usually then burst into obligatory floods of tears, proclaiming that this was their one and only dream and there is nothing else they can do.

We should not put our eggs all in one basket, so to speak. If you pin all your hopes on one dream, you might be missing out on something fantastic that you should be doing that would be far more fulfilling. Your soul does not give a fig whether you are the next Alicia Keys, or not. All your soul cares about is your spiritual growth.

I once wanted to go into advertising and although I applied for some jobs, I did not try as hard as I could have. I was almost afraid of getting a job in the industry. Some self-help wizard might have told me that my fear was holding me back in life, but the reality was that it helped me. I realised, eventually, that I would have abhorred a job in advertising because I would have had to compromise my ethics and well-being, to work in that industry.

Not long after, I met a remarkable man who changed my life, I discovered my intuition, found true happiness and the rest is history. If you are afraid of going for that dream job, you need to establish whether that fear is your intuition saying, "Stay away" or your insecurities, saying, "You are not capable." If it is your intuition, then you need to listen to that voice and only chase something that feels one hundred per cent right for you. If you chase it and it is not right for you, it will stall your personal development and happiness.

You might be wondering why some fears are even on the rational list, such as: a fear of bread, having children and a fear of cancer. These fears are entirely rational. If you are allergic to bread and it is going to cause anaphylactic shock if you eat it, that fear is rational. That fear will prevent you from doing something that would harm you and you will hopefully endeavour to seek alternatives.

It is not the end of the world if you cannot eat bread. There are plenty of other options. I have seen people who have been told they must not drink caffeine due to an illness proclaim, that they cannot possibly give it up. Why on earth not? One lady exclaimed that caffeine was her only pleasure in life. We have to remember that many of us in the Western world are very affluent compared to the rest of the world. We should be appreciative of what we have. With regards to food, we should eat to live and not live to eat. The world is not going to spontaneously combust if we cannot indulge in all our fancies. Try to see the positive side and all the lessons that should be gleaned from life, rather than wallowing in the perceived sacrifices you have had to make.

Fear of having children if you live in an unhappy, unstable environment is a perfectly understandable fear. This fear protects the unborn child and it protects you. There are some people who seem to think that they must have children, that having children forms part of the reason we are here on this earth. If they do not have children, they feel empty and lacking. If you are not happy without a child, you will not be happy with one. You need to be happy within yourself not as a result of something you have, whether it is a physical object or another human being.

A child is not a buttress to fill your emotional void. If you bring a child into this world and give it an inadequate life because of your circumstances, you have done a disservice to the child and a disservice to yourself. It is better to wait until you have a more stable environment to have children. You might never have children in this lifetime. Again, it is not the end of the world as we know it, if you do not. Not having children will not make you a lesser or greater person. Only the way you live your life, can do that.

My final example is the fear of having cancer because family members have had this illness. This fear is furnishing you with the opportunity to change your life for the better. Perhaps both your mother and your grandmother had breast cancer. If they did, your risk of developing this illness will be dramatically increased. Of course you are going to be scared, but there are actions you can take to minimise your own risk of contracting cancer. There are lessons you can learn that will foster your personal and spiritual development.

Look at the positive changes you can make in your life. You can change your whole lifestyle to a healthier one. You can consume healthier and more nourishing foods that fight free radicals and avoid dangers like smoking and heavy drinking. You can try complementary therapies to minimise your stress and enhance your overall well-being. Your life can become happier and richer because of the positive steps you have taken and you can share the lessons you have learned to help others who are in the same predicament.

So, as you can see, there are plenty of things you can do to prevent rational fears from becoming overwhelming. They are not halting your true potential, but giving you a little nudge to point you in the right direction. Be happy that you have rational fears and then take steps to prevent potential negative consequences.

Irrational Fears

Many of our irrational fears are a product of our loss of direction in life and a distinct lack of, or a very weak intuitive connection. Some of our irrational fears are caused by buried emotional traumas or by our upbringing, environment and conditioning, which lead to a fractured intuitive connection. Such fears are born out of our physical and emotional bodies and not from our intuition.

With our irrational fears, the root cause of the issue or issues always needs to be addressed. Many of the irrational fears I have cited in the box example can be attributed to a combination of factors and can be resolved by establishing a powerful intuitive connection and dealing with any emotional causes.

When we lack intuition, we feel incredibly lost and afraid, because the world becomes a very lonely place. We look for solace, where solace cannot be found. In vain, we try to fill the void, but it can only be made complete by one thing, a bond with our souls.

Without the unconditional love and awareness of our higher selves, we flounder around helplessly. Any appearance of control is an illusion, because it only extends to a physical world and in reality that control, will not last and it can be withdrawn, at any one moment, by the Universe. Life minus the union with our souls is lifeless, unfathomable and scary.

Our emotional traumas hold us back from achieving our true potential. They prevent us from being our real selves and cloud our true insight and judgement. We think we know who we are and we pronounce, "You cannot change me, this is just the way I am," when in truth, the image we portray is a far cry from the nature of our souls. We act according to the situation we are in and there are very few people whom we allow to witness our true nature. We desperately need to clear these traumas away, so that we are free of the heavy burden that prevents us from progressing physically, emotionally and spiritually.

The fear of trusting in our intuition typically arises because we are afraid of taking responsibility for our lives and we fear the guilt that will arise as a result of the actions we have taken in our lives. We would often rather ignore the guilt. We are also afraid that it will bring up questions that we do not know how to answer. Furthermore, it will force us to question our lives and the roots of our very existence. As the adage goes, ignorance is bliss and we would sometimes rather wallow in it than become more aware.

Awareness results in us having to follow our intuition and make the right choices, because we can no longer make excuses for ourselves. We perceive that ignorance makes for an easier way of life. We can proclaim, "You only live once," and partake in a whole range of activities that are devastating to our spiritual and personal growth, under the illusion that there are no consequences for our actions. It means that no matter what happens to us in life, we never have to put any effort into making the correct choices. I have heard so many stories of individuals who deliberately choose to ignore their better judgement and I am sure you have too.

I know of people, who have had lung cancer, then had a lung removed and they continued to smoke cigarettes. An individual may develop cancer and say, "What the hell, I am going to enjoy my life while I can." *Enjoying* their life, may entail going out partying to all hours, consuming anything that takes their fancy, regardless of whether it is exacerbating their ill health or not and generally continuing past lifestyle patterns in reckless defiance. This is far easier than facing up to the truth, than sitting down and thinking, "How have I personally contributed to my illness? What is this teaching me? How can I make things better?"

Practically every experience in life is an opportunity for personal growth, for us, or those around us. If we get an illness we should instead be saying to ourselves, "How can I change my lifestyle for the better?" We should be looking towards our own spiritual growth and personal development and asking ourselves what we could learn from our many and varied experiences.

This is not just the case for illness and health, but for any area of our lives. We are scared to face up to the truth, but the truth is there to help us and those around us, to learn and to become better individuals. Our intuition is nothing to be afraid of. It offers us peace and everlasting happiness and what is so scary about that?

We sometimes think that we will open up a can of worms if we trust our intuition. We often believe that we do not deserve true happiness. There are some things we have to face up to at some point in our lives, it is inevitable and it helps us to learn and to grow. Once we do face up to those things, we move onto bigger, better and more spiritual things.

Our intuition should not be looked upon as a can of worms, but a beautiful and magnificent journey. If we are completely devoid of intuition, then we should be afraid. If we have intuition, we should embrace it. Our true spiritual paths are so much more exquisite than the ones we create on earth.

We love and long to have control in our lives, or at least to appear to have control. It makes us feel nice, safe and secure. We are afraid of relinquishing any of that control. It gives us a great sense of purpose and power over our lives. We often try *so* hard to control the direction of our lives that we lose sight of our intuition and we lose our spiritual paths. We are sure that we are in complete control, but in reality, we are on a wayward spiral out of control.

The thing to realise is that we are all subject to the laws of the Universe. There are *some* things we do have *some* control over, but the method for attaining true happiness and spiritual growth is to let go and let the Universe be our guide. We need to make good choices, follow our intuition and let the Universe do the rest. You will find that once you simply allow the Universe to guide you, life will become much more fluid, simple and easier to digest.

We need to be accepting of what the Universe has in store for us. The more accepting we become, the more we are able to adapt and trust our own inner wisdom. This offers true peace of mind. Then, we can genuinely comprehend that everything will be as it should. Surrendering control is a huge fear for many people, but letting go of that desire to control everything is a gargantuan relief, a weight off your shoulders. Accepting is so rewarding and so enlightening.

The more you try to control your life, the more the Universe will seize that control. If you listen to the Universe some of it will be given back to you, but only to a degree. Everything that happens must happen in a particular way and it will do so whether you attempt to control it or not. So the answer is very plain and simple. Just let go. Once you release the control, the fear of losing control will dissipate because you will reach a higher state of awareness.

One of the biggest irrational fears that human beings possess, is the fear of being alone. We surround ourselves with people because it alleviates some of our destituteness, but does it really? You can be in a crowded room and still feel lonely. You can be the life and soul of the party and feel utterly alone. Life is not about how many friends we have or what our social circle is like. Life is about pursuing our higher paths on earth. We can only ever find true contentment if we are treading those paths. Everything else is peripheral.

Loneliness can never be completely vanquished until we accept that we are not alone, not because we have friends, acquaintances or family around us, but because we have the constant presence of God, Divine energy, or whatever label you see fit to use. We are surrounded by unconditional love and if you stop, take stock and sit quietly for long enough you cannot help but feel it.

There is nothing wrong with being around others if you are around people that foster your personal growth, but you should not *need* to be around other people to feel happy or complete. If you cannot be happy being by yourself, then you are not really happy. Furthermore, there is no use being around people who are detrimental to your self-development. These people will zap your energy and try to make you feel as terrible as they do. By doing this, they can feel safe in the knowledge that they are not the only one mired in misery and that temporarily helps to soothe some of their own personal fears. Be around people who lift you, not around people who drag you down and remember that we are never alone, no matter how much we might feel that we are.

Another principal irrational fear is the fear of being judged by others. You may perceive this as rational because people can have a tendency to judge. However, what others think of us is completely meaningless. All that matters is that we are undertaking our true purpose in life and taking steps towards the Divine.

We are here to follow our paths, we are not here to serve other people or bow to their demands. We are not here to please others. People may cast judgements, but they wield no power to judge. If you are popular with other people, but you are not pursuing your spiritual path, your popularity is entirely insignificant. It might mean something now, in your physical body, in a physical world, but to the overall journey of your soul, which is infinite, it means nothing. You embody poverty. If you have few people around you and few friends, but you are traversing your spiritual path and taking heed of your intuition, you have everything. You have wealth beyond human measure.

There are a plethora of irrational fears, too many to mention, so I will discuss two more very widely held fears: the fear of God and the fear of death.

Some religions have carefully constructed a God of vengeance and wrath, a God that instils us mere mortals with unmitigated fear. So it goes we should stick strictly to precise and rigid codes, through fear of God's almighty power that could strike us down into the depths of a fiery Hell, in any second now. This fear is created to ensure that people stick to the unyielding instructions of that particular religion. It is not about God, it is about keeping people in line, under the influence of their religious leaders. It has more to do with the human lust for control than God.

God is nothing to be afraid of. God loves us all. God loves us when we know no love ourselves. God loves us, though we love him not and despite our many shortcomings. It is the actions of human beings that are terrifying. If we are going to be afraid of something, we would do better to be afraid of mortals than of God. Human beings are capable of such deplorable and grave deeds as murder, taking innocent lives and abominable acts of torture and gross indecency. We take lives all the time, without even thinking about it. Many human beings do not value their own species, or any other. On the contrary, God loves everything unconditionally. God is a love that knows no bounds. Forget the religious God, feel the real God.

Quite similarly, death is nothing to fear. The fear of death is ingrained in us from a very early age by our culture, society, upbringing and conditioning. We have come to see death as the end. As the world has become more physical and humanity has steered astray from its spiritual path, the earthly realm has become a beginning and an end in itself. In truth, it is simply part of a cycle. We are composed of energy and energy never dies.

We try to stay younger longer, we are living longer and some people would like to inhabit this earth forever. If a pill was released tomorrow that promised eternal human life, millions, if not more would be queuing up for their shot at human immortality. I would proclaim them to be imprudent because as souls, as energies we are so much more complete than when tied down in a body, in a dark and failing world.

This life we have here on earth is but a snapshot of our entire journeys. It is a very important snapshot that has implications for the rest of our souls' existence, but it is so exceedingly short. We should not view death as an end, but as a beginning.

People mourn over the loss of their dearly departed but really they mourn for their own loss. The deceased have just taken leave of this world, they are not dead. The people left behind feel profound sadness because they feel they have lost someone they deeply loved. Death is nothing to be afraid of. The enlightened do not fear death, because they have awareness of what their afterlife brings. As we become more intuitive, we escape that needless fear of the cessation of our own mortality. We are all going to die from this fragile earth whether we fear it or not, so why be afraid?

As you progress on your true path, through your own self-development, your irrational fears will steadily dissolve. There is no quick fix or easy way to allay these fears. Their dissolution comes only from you walking your spiritual path and absorbing and acting on every whisper and word of your intuition.

Only One Win-Win

Sometimes, we would like to believe that we can choose any path we want in life, that we can fashion our own destiny. In reality, our paths are heavily guided by the Universe and we are all heading for our final destinations. We have choices to make along the way. How we use those choices, determines our happiness, well-being and our soul paths. Those choices are vital. We have a path to walk and we can walk that path in a straight line, or we can go in a zigzag, or we can go up and down and then back up again (a limited number of times), or we can reverse down the path, veer off on the other one and never attain any personal or spiritual growth whatsoever. We do not have unlimited paths and unlimited choices, but we choose *how* we walk our paths.

Now, are those choices good or bad? That depends on our destiny. You will notice that above, I said "veer off on the other one." There are two distinct paths in life that we can choose from: one that steers us in the correct direction towards becoming more evolved beings – a spiritual path and one that propels us in the other direction, reversing or halting our emotional and spiritual progress – a physical path. For some of our lives, we can walk with a foot on each path but at some point we have to choose which path we will take and stick to it. Some self-help 'gurus' try to lead us into believing that we can take any path we want in life, with only positive results. Sorry to burst the bubble, but if you fail to trust your intuition, if you voyage down the physical route of chasing physical or emotional desires, the repercussions might not be what you had hoped for.

We should not fool ourselves into believing that we can take any course of action in life and expect only good to come our way. If our intuition tells us to do one thing and we do the exact opposite, then we cannot realistically suppose that everything in our lives will be plain sailing. We might get some more chances to make the right choices for our paths, but ultimately if we do not make those right choices, if we do not take the spiritual path, we cannot expect to come up smelling of roses.

It is essential to make choices in life that are right for your path and for your intuition. Your soul wants you to make the right choices, the ones that take you closer to the Universe or God. It wants you to take the choices that steer you towards unconditional love, rather than tearing you away from it. I feel that it is reckless to believe that we can live our lives in any way we desire, without negative consequences. Call it Karma if you will, in line with the Buddhist and Hindu interpretation, that our actions breed inevitable consequences for us, either good or bad, in this life or the next life. The adverse results, as this would suggest, may not form part of our current lifetime, but I thoroughly believe that it affects our souls' overall journeys.

Even if you only believe in the lives we lead here on earth, surely it is better to make worthy choices that benefit ourselves and others, not just in a physical or emotional way, but also in a spiritual way.

There is no need to shy away from the term spiritual. Being spiritual does not have to be an esoteric term. It means living your life in the right way and acting and thinking in the right way. Spirituality has nothing to do with what you wear, what so called 'spiritual' objects you buy, whether you call yourself spiritual or not or whether you claim to be a spiritual teacher.

There are many individuals who claim to be spiritual without even truly knowing what that means and many who shirk the term spiritual whilst constantly living a spiritual life. If you determinedly trust and follow your intuition, if you do not rest on your laurels but persistently strive to be a better person, if you are taking steps in the right direction, if you are humble in the face of the Universe, then you are spiritual. Spirituality is not a consumer item, however hard society tries to make it so.

If you choose to walk the right path, then you will be less inclined to fall prey to irrational fears and your rational fears will not oppress you, because you will take heed of them. If you choose to walk the other path, then that is your choice, but do not complain about the consequences and the prevalence of irrational fears. These come as standard when you perpetually and deliberately flout your intuitive guidance. This is the way of the Universe. You can choose win-win or lose-lose. The diagram on the following page demonstrates this concept.

Win-Win, Lose-Lose

Spiritual path - Win-Win

❑ **Trusting your intuition.**
❑ **Making the right choices.**
❑ **Allowing the Universe to take its course.**
❑ **Accepting your true purpose.**
❑ **Serving your true purpose.**

Physical Path - Lose-Lose

❑ **Pursuing purely physical desires.**
❑ **Making the wrong choices.**
❑ **Trying to bend the will of the Universe.**
❑ **Flouting your intuition.**
❑ **Serving your whims.**

Rise above it, or sink down to the depths. We choose. There is only one win-win in this life, or any other life and that is the pursuit of our spiritual paths. Whatever you decide to do, you need to be aware of all the consequences and accept the consequences that those choices bring. For every action there is a consequence. Before you leap headfirst into anything, consider the repercussions first.

You might want to be a company director but before you go for that position, remember these things: you will probably be working long hours, you will be under a lot of stress, you may not get to spend a great deal of time with your family and although your family will probably complain about this, they will be accustomed to a certain standard of living and will be expecting you to maintain that standard of living.

If you want to be self-employed, remember that you will need to be motivated, you will have to work long hours and take fewer holidays because you will not be getting paid for them. There may be times when business is slow and you will fret about your finances. Again, your family may become resentful because you are not spending much time with them.

Perhaps you want to be a recording artist. Be aware that it is a difficult industry to break into, you will probably spend a lot of time getting nowhere fast and you may have to undertake gigs in smoky bars, for very little income. If you do get a record contract, you might have to sacrifice some of your integrity to get to the top. People may take advantage of you and pander to your ego just because of who you are. You could have very few true friends and you will constantly be in the public eye. Close personal relationships could be difficult to establish because you are constantly touring. People will see you as an artist rather than seeing behind the facade and your fans will expect you to live up to that ideal. The press will bring you up, only to take you down again.

These are just a few examples to give you an idea of the sort of consequences people can expect to face with any given choice they make. If you are not prepared to live with the consequences, then make a different choice. Think long and hard about where you take yourself in life. Some of these consequences could also be viewed as rational fears, so you need to trust your intuition before jumping into anything. If it does not sit quite right, there is probably a good reason for this.

Take your time with making decisions. Only make an impulsive decision if you are one hundred per cent making that choice through intuition, rather than through physical or emotional desires. If you kid yourself that it is an intuitive choice when it is not, you will be subject to the consequences of that decision. Either you need to learn to live with it and not complain about it, or accept that it was a mistake and try to make better choices the next time round.

Circles of Life

It is a philosophy of the founder of the therapy I practise, known as Usui Reiki and a philosophy of mine, that we all have three 'bodies', so to speak. The first is a physical body – driven by physical desires, the second an emotional body – driven by emotional desires and often crutches and a spiritual body – driven by Divine will or the will of the Universe, if you prefer. I believe that these three bodies are all made up of energy, with our less tangible spiritual bodies vibrating at the highest frequencies and our physical bodies vibrating at the lowest frequencies. When we are born, these three bodies reside in perfect harmony. Our intuition is strong and firmly guides our other two bodies in the appropriate ways for our journeys on earth. The frequencies of all our bodies are high.

As we live our lives and almost inevitably become conditioned by society, parents, peers and others, these three bodies that previously held fast can begin to disconnect and drift apart. Children are vary rarely encouraged to embrace their intuition and higher spiritual nature and are sometimes reprimanded for doing so.

Our societies are, for the most part, fuelled by the pursuit of physical desires, materialism and consumerism. Many children are unable to detach themselves from this way of life because it is all they have ever known and it hard for anyone to extricate themselves from it.

Throughout their childhood, teenage years and then adulthood many people experience a myriad of emotional traumas. Children learn from the actions and behaviours of their parents and from the attitudes of the majority. As this takes its toll, the three bodies that were once in a blissful union begin to lose their ability to successfully communicate with one another. We become largely governed by the lower frequencies of our physical and emotional bodies. Our souls try to communicate through intuition, but the further these three bodies drift apart, the more difficult this becomes.

Our physical bodies sharply shove us in the direction of hankering after earthly desires. We wish for more and more money, the latest products, physical satisfaction, fame, glory, pampered egos and such like. As a result, we become unreasonably angry, frustrated, greedy, perhaps gluttonous and hateful, slaves to our physical aspirations.

Our emotional bodies want to be loved, but very often they have not experienced unconditional love and so yearn to be needed and wanted. The same tired old messages play over and over again in our minds; I wish everyone would like me, please like me, why don't they like me? They are judging me. There must be something wrong with me. What is wrong with me? Why am I never happy? Perhaps, if I was in a relationship I would be happy. I am in a relationship and I am still not happy. The world is awful. It's everybody else's fault or is it my fault? Why didn't he love me? Why didn't she love me? What is wrong with me? I wish everyone would like me...and so on.

Our significantly distorted concept of love is largely based on our upbringing, culture and environment. Our love is predominantly conditional. Our emotions are not governed and directed by our souls, so they shoot off all over the place, lacking the knowledge of our intuition to guide us in the right direction.

Sometimes, our decidedly clingy emotional bodies become firmly attached to physical things because they find it much easier to form a dialogue with our physical bodies than our drifting away spiritual bodies. The frequencies are closer, facilitating this outcome.

Some people become highly emotional about their possessions or treat people like possessions. We then get the manipulating tears and the 'poor me' syndrome.

As human beings, we tend to judge ourselves on how we look, what we are wearing, how successful our careers are, how much money we have, where we live, what kind of a relationship we are in, what possessions we have. We judge other people by the same token. If we feel we are falling below the mark, we become depressed and riddled with self-pity, rarely stopping to consider what we have to be grateful for.

Rather than considering how our own actions might be contributing to our state of mind and well-being, we shirk taking personal responsibility in favour of placing the blame elsewhere. We ask, "Why does this person see me in this way?" rather than asking, "How am I behaving to make them see me in this way?" We look outwards for answers, rather than inwards. We come to lack everything when we think we **have** everything.

Strong characters in search of power usually rise to the top, the ones that constantly strive to caress their huge egos, longing for adulation, eminence and the tools that will further their physical ambitions. These are the ones that play on our emotions, weaknesses and our own burgeoning, physically driven egos.

Meanwhile, our poor intuition, our poor spiritual bodies are floundering. They desperately try to make contact with our physical and emotional bodies, but we can either no longer hear their pleas or perhaps, we choose not to. In a state of denial, we march on obtusely through life. If we have managed to maintain some level of communication with our spiritual bodies, we occasionally hear them, distantly in the far reaches of our minds. If all discourse has been severed, we cannot hear them at all.

Those with no connection to their spiritual bodies will chase after bigger, cheaper and more hedonistic thrills, because the last ones never quite hit the spot. The drink was not enough so the drugs did the trick. The drugs then wore off so a few hollow sexual relationships gave a confidence booster. Then that got boring too, so it was time to move onto a new, more dangerous titilation. You get the picture. What our physical and emotional bodies are really pining for is the unconditional love that comes from our souls and our souls' Divine connection. In its absence, these two bodies seek similar feelings elsewhere, but they never quite manage to get there.

The vicious cycle ploughs on. Some manage to break free from it, but many do not. We kid ourselves we are happy, when we do not know what happiness is, we kid ourselves we are in love, when we do not know what love feels like. We want everything that was never intended for us and want nothing that we truly need and blithely, we wallow in indifference and resigned apathy to our current state of affairs. A lack of connection prevents us from seeing beyond the ends of our own noses. We worry about everything, apart from the lost connection we should be worrying about. We fear without understanding our fears. Life is sometimes fun and it is sometimes numb, but never, truly happy.

Not everyone loses their spiritual connection. Some people, despite tumultuous lives still retain that bond with their intuition, if not all the time then at least some of the time, they listen to their inner guidance. Certain people still have some kind of spiritual bond, but the majority of the time they ignore their wise inner voice and frequently look to others for wisdom rather than trusting their own.

Others are so disconnected from their intuition and even emotional bodies that they lack all love and compassion for themselves or anyone else. All they seek are physical desires and excitements, however horrific they appear to the rest of society. They will hurt someone without a thought or care for the consequences and if not others, they will hurt themselves, lacking any self-love whatsoever. So the cycle of lives continue; highs and lows but mostly very lacking.

If we can manage to re-conflate the bond that was broken, or if not broken, severely hindered, we can change our lives for the better, follow the wisdom of our Divine inner guidance and learn the beauty of a real inner peace and contentment that no person on this planet can shake. If we dare to strive for the sake of our souls, for the sake of each other's souls, we can re-kindle the bond that held us so perfect in our newborn state. If we do not, we will never break the cycle. So why not break it today. Start by learning the difference between your rational and irrational fears.

The techniques at the end of this chapter will help you to achieve this, by first of all, cultivating your intuitive connection. When you are able to be more intuitive, you will be better able to understand and deal with your fears. For too long, we have given poor old fear a rough deal. We have whinged and whined about our fears without understanding how we can cope with or quell them. Before you try to chuck your fear in the nearest trash can, give it a chance to show you something meteoric. Sift the rational from the irrational fears and work out your action plan to make your life truly worth living.

"Fear has its use but cowardice has none."

Mahatma Gandhi

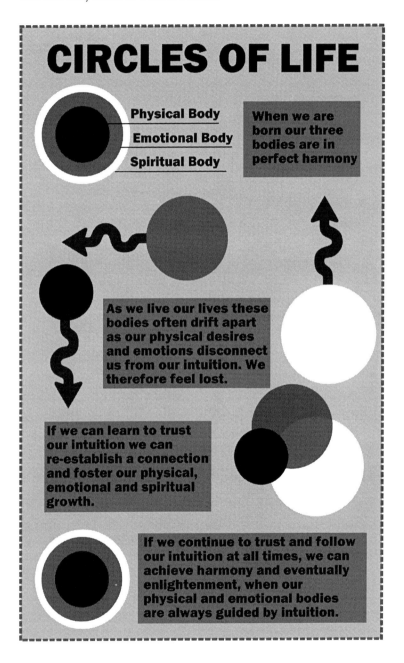

CIRCLES OF LIFE

Physical Body
Emotional Body
Spiritual Body

When we are born our three bodies are in perfect harmony

As we live our lives these bodies often drift apart as our physical desires and emotions disconnect us from our intuition. We therefore feel lost.

If we can learn to trust our intuition we can re-establish a connection and foster our physical, emotional and spiritual growth.

If we continue to trust and follow our intuition at all times, we can achieve harmony and eventually enlightenment, when our physical and emotional bodies are always guided by intuition.

Techniques

Where Is My Intuition?

 Grab yourself a piece of paper and a pen and write down a list of things that are true and untrue about yourself. Mix them up. There is no need to separate these items.

 Read the list out to yourself very slowly and notice how it feels when you read out a fact and a lie. Read your list out several times.

 Read out the list again, but this time after each fact say to yourself, "This is a lie," and after each lie say to yourself, "This is true." If you cannot bring yourself to say the opposite of your statement, then that is your intuition stopping your from doing it. If you can say the opposite, notice how it makes you feel when you tell the truth and when you tell lies.

Practise this exercise a few times a week.

Focus Your Mind

❑ You can do this exercise almost anywhere, whether you are on the bus or train, at work, at home in front of the TV, or if you prefer, in your own quiet space. Sit down comfortably with your back straight and rest your palms facing upwards in your lap.

❑ Breathe in and out very slowly and deeply, through your nose, for a few seconds and keep your eyes closed.

❑ On the next in breath, visualise pure white light coming down from above you and into the crown of your head.

❑ As you gently hold your breath for ten seconds, visualise the light form into a bright white globe, centred mid-forehead (third eye), on the inside of your head.

❑ As you breathe out, continue to maintain the visualisation of the globe and push a beam of light from that globe, all the way down to your heart area.

❑ Hold your breath for ten seconds and whilst still maintaining the image of the globe inside your head, visualise another globe of light forming in your heart area, getting bigger and brighter.

❑ As you breathe in, continue to maintain the visualisations of the other two globes and push a beam of light from the heart globe all the way down to your navel area.

❑ As you hold your breath for ten seconds, visualise a white globe forming in your navel area and see that globe getting bigger and brighter.

❑ As you breathe out, visualise the three globes being pushed out of your body and back into the Universe, one at a time, starting with the navel globe, then the heart globe then the head globe.

❑ Repeat the process between one and five times.

Be Intuitive

❑   Sit down comfortably, either on the chair, or on the floor if you prefer. Start to breathe very slowly in through your nose and out through your nose, becoming aware of the feeling of the passage of air as it passes into your nostrils and out of your nostrils.

❑   After an in breath, hold your breath and using the middle finger of your right hand pat the centre of your forehead, between your eyebrows, three times.

❑   As you breathe out, switch over to the index finger of your right hand and gently rub the same area, three times in an anti- clockwise direction.

❑   Breathe in again and repeat the above two processes. Repeat this entire process between three and twenty five times.

❑   Once you have finished, press your middle finger of your left hand on the same area of your forehead and silently say with meaning and purpose, "May I gain the wisdom to trust my intuition."

❑   Take a deep breath in and out to finish and silently thank your intuition and Universal guidance.

Toss A Coin

 Think of some questions about your life that have been troubling you, that have an either / or option, that you are willing to follow through with. Grab yourself a piece of paper and a pen and write a few of them down.

 Get hold of a coin (any one will do). You are going to toss the coin, heads for one answer, tails for the other, but first you are going to guess intuitively what the answer will be. Mentally ask your intuition to help you and if you like you can ask for Universal guidance.

 Make a note of how many you guessed correctly and what the correct answers were and keep hold of the information.

 Three times a week repeat the process until you get it right every time. Starting to recognise your intuition now?

"Where ignorance is our master, there is no possibility of real peace."

The Dalai Lama

Material Success And Spiritual Success Do Not Equate...

...because the pursuit of money is not spiritual

A Tall Tale

Scenario One

Every day on the bus to work, I sat completely engrossed in a book. This particular one talked at length about abundance; how material success could easily be mine if I followed a few golden rules. I was so pleased to hear that amassing wealth could be a spiritual activity. It had not occurred to me before, but now it made perfect sense. All that was left to do was to get started on my big plans and to believe that they would really work. So the next day, I went out and bought a lottery ticket. I had bought one before, but this time it was different because I believed. I carefully chose the numbers and waited for the day to arrive when the big win would fall into my lap.

It did not happen. What can I say; I did not even get one lousy number. I am so disappointed. Still, if I really think hard about it, I have a lot to be grateful for. I have my health, a roof over my head, food to eat and a loving family. I came to the conclusion that these things are more important. Sure money helps to pay the bills but it can't make you spiritually happy. I guess I got far too hung up on my goal of monetary success and I liked the idea that this could be combined with a spiritual path.

I suppose in a way the two might coincide, but in my humble opinion it is better to call a spade a spade. Chasing money is not at all spiritual, it is a physical pursuit and it is foolish for us to kid ourselves otherwise.

Scenario Two

Every day on the bus to work, I sat completely engrossed in a book. This particular one talked at length about abundance; how material success could easily be mine if I followed a few golden rules. I was so pleased to hear that amassing wealth could be a spiritual activity. It had not occurred to me before, but now it made perfect sense. All that was left to do was to get started on my big plans and to believe that they would really work. So the next day, I went out and bought a lottery ticket. I had bought one before, but this time it was different because I believed. I carefully chose the numbers and waited for the day to arrive when the big win would fall into my lap.

I actually did it! I won the lottery. I made all these big plans. I shared some with my family and friends. I bought a nice big house. I even got myself some waiting and cleaning staff. I threw lavish parties and made a whole new bunch of friends. I set out on a new business venture selling household products. I went on so many holidays abroad. Still, despite all this, something was missing. The dream I had envisaged did not live up to reality. I found that more and more individuals were drawn to me, purely because of what I had. Sure, I had everything anyone could possibly ever want, but I felt empty inside. Even giving some of my money away to charity did not make me feel any better about myself.

It came to me one sleepless night. I did not have any kind of spiritual connection. I got so caught up with chasing and spending money, that I completely lost my spirituality. I realised then that the quest for money has nothing to do with spirituality, it is a physical pursuit and it is foolish for us to kid ourselves otherwise.

Seriously Though...

Money can buy you a great many things, but it can never buy you spirituality. There are a plethora of self-help books that tie money making into spiritual concepts. If individuals want to make money, fine that is their choice, we all need to earn a living, but finding success on a material level is not spiritual. It is physical.

However hard we try to dress it up, we cannot stick square pegs into round holes, well, unless we batter them around a bit and try to make them kind of fit, of a fashion, but not really. Then we can pretend that they fitted all along and say, "Making money can be a spiritual pursuit. Reach for all your material goals. Put it out to the Universe that your dream is to win the lottery, or be a high flyer, entrepreneur or anything you want." The Universe does not work that way. It does not exist to give us what we want, it exists to teach us lessons and to give us what we need (which is rarely what we wanted, if we lack a profound intuitive connection).

Making money is not inherently bad in itself, but it has absolutely nothing to do with spirituality, which revolves around how you live your life. Some people say that by giving you become more spiritual, but again, that depends on how you live your life. You could be someone with a low income who gives some of your earnings to charity; you could be a millionaire who gives a vast amount of money to charity, or somewhere in between. This can of course be construed as a worthy act, but you could give away *all* of your wealth and still live your life in the wrong way. Giving is not a spiritual act unless it accompanies a spiritual way of life. Giving from the right place is a wonderful thing. Giving from the wrong place is a hollow thing.

There are some incredibly spiritually lacking people in the world who give away a part of their fortune. There are some very spiritual people in the world who give away a part of their fortune, but they are spiritual because right living, right thinking and right actions pervade every avenue of their lives. Their thoughts, choices and actions are governed by intuition. They do not try to fool themselves into believing that by giving some of what they own, they can sit back and do nothing else.

Giving can be entirely meaningless. Like many things in the world of the twenty-first century, giving has becoming a vapid ritual. We give gifts and cards at Christmas, birthdays and other occasions, but why do we do it? Often we do it purely because it is the done thing. In reality, many of these occasions are a consumer sham. We go out and have dinner with our partners on Valentines Day and perhaps buy them a bunch of roses. We should be loving and emotionally giving with our partners all of the time, not just on one day. If we truly love each other, we do not need to buy gifts because we know that on the grand scale of things, it isn't that important. Our unconditional love and respect should be enough. If our love is conditional, then we obsess about giving gifts because we feel guilty and thus we allay some of our guilt by making pointless gestures.

I am not proclaiming that we should completely give up gift giving, but that we should recognise that it does not make us spiritual as individuals. The two can be poles apart. Of course, there are people living in terrible conditions that desperately need financial help. We can help a small amount, but not enough to make a real difference. It is governments that have the power to do something about this, but they choose not to.

The only thing we, as individuals, need to be giving is our unconditional love to one another and to every living thing. Whether that love means disciplining our children to help them learn, dishing out some harsh truths to help others learn, giving a hug or listening to someone to let them know you care, staying away from someone to teach them a lesson, caring for and not harming animals, looking after the earth, living for our spiritual paths. These are the things that are really important, not gifts. Money is necessary for us to live, because we live in an economic world, but it is no more than printed paper. It is an object. We do not really own it because we cannot take it with us.

Spiritual success has absolutely nothing to do with money, with what we earn, what jobs we have, what cars we have, or whatever physical achievements we have notched up throughout our lives. If we want to make money and it is within the remit of our paths, then we can make money, but making money should never be the goal, it should be a by-product. If making money *is* the goal, then we need to re-evaluate our lives and our priorities.

There are many things in life that are so much more important than being rich. We cannot draft up a list for the Universe of what we desire and then realistically expect it to come knocking at our door. The Universe is not an ordering service, where you can ask for whatever takes your fancy. I believe that it is exceptionally awry to ask the Universe for material successes, or a holiday in France, or a new house, a new partner, or a new job. It demonstrates a distinct lack of respect for the Universe and lack of an intuitive connection. We should allow the Universe to be our guide and graciously accept what we are given. If we live wisely and judiciously and if we trust our intuition we will be given more, but it will not necessarily be material wealth, it will be spiritual wealth. It may sound trite but spiritual wealth is worth more than all the money in the world.

Too many people are looking for easy answers. They do not want to work hard for anything or wait for anything. Instead they expect it to instantaneously drop into their lap whenever they express their demands. Their physical bodies are controlling their thoughts and actions. I believe that this is the wrong way to live our lives. We need to work hard, be accepting, be patient and take the time to be still. If we can achieve this, we will be given what we need in good time and we will be grateful for what we have received, rather than continually peeking around the corner for a new frivolity.

Besides, who says we are all meant to rich anyway? If governments chose to share our material wealth as nations, then everyone could have enough money to live comfortably, without needing to be materially wealthy. It is a nice thought, but just a thought. It is highly unlikely to ever occur. Some of us will be rich and some of us will not. If we do not become rich, we should not constantly beat ourselves up about it, but instead count our blessings.

Money can **only** bring physical happiness and, of course, security. If you are poor and spiritually unfulfilled and come into money, you will be rich and spiritually unfulfilled. If you are poor and spiritually content and come into material wealth, you will be rich and spiritually content.

Money does not define who you are as an individual. Bling draped around your neck does not make you superior to anyone else. You can be rich, strut around and lord it up and make everyone else around you feel small and envious of what you own. You can purchase diamonds, pearls and lavish possessions. You can even give money to charity to give the appearance of doing something worthy. On a Universal level though, you are no better than anyone else. In fact if you are living such a life, then they are better than you.

You can be materially rich and choose not to parade around like a peacock showing off your worldly wealth, but put money in its place, remain humble and always listen to your intuition. On a Universal level, you are a spiritual person and your money is just a physical aspect of your life that does not control your life. You give then, because you genuinely want to help people and do not need to brag to anyone about it, because you are secure in yourself.

Another thing to be aware of is that money can bring with it a whole range of negative emotions if you are not spiritually sound to begin with. Once you get a taste for the green stuff, it may take you over. Your overriding ambition could metamorphose into piling up more and more money. If you decide to become a director in a big corporation you may have to sacrifice some of your standards and ethics to earn that money. Some of your morals may go right out the window.

Money can do some very strange things to people. It has this extraordinary ability to bring out unrestrained avarice and megalomania and the karma for this kind of behaviour will be nothing to celebrate about. As I have said previously, making money should be a by product and not the main goal. In reality, you need to be in a sound place spiritually before you make your fortune. This way, the money will not change you, or pull you away from personal growth.

Again, remember that you cannot take your money with you when you die. Money and the power it brings are fleeting and it only lasts for as long as we last in our human shells. We have to live in a physical world. We need money to live. It is undoubtedly nice to be able to live comfortably and without vexing about where the next cent or penny is coming from. If you have a huge fortune and you are wise, you may be able to use that money in a genuine and self-less way to the benefit of others. But, when all is said and done, how much money you do or do not have means squat in the big scheme of things.

Abundance

There is a theory that supposes that whatever you give, you will receive. If you give others recognition, respect and love, you will receive this in return. Some self-help experts dare to apply this theory to the 'art' of money making. Quick, let me stand aloft the nearest multiplex and chuck out some coinage at the unsuspecting passers by. I used to do that when I was a child, hugely entertained by the shocked civilians below, who felt the sharp pang of pennies bouncing off their bonces. Funnily enough, they were not impressed and nor, I doubt, was the Universe.

Back to reality, we need to be offering unconditional love, but that does not always mean showering people with praise, respect, adoration, recognition and such like. What is more, giving something does not mean that you are going to get it back. It might get shoved back in your face. As I am sure I have mentioned before, unconditional love can mean standing back, letting people fight their own battles in life, not affording them with respect because they do not deserve any.

Unconditional love is not always nice, sometimes it is tough. Sometimes, unconditional love can be a bitter pill that other people need to swallow and the truth is written on the medicine bottle. In more serious terms, unconditional love is about understanding the truth and helping people in the right way according to that truth. It is about helping their souls even if it does not seem to be helping their flesh.

Respect should be given to those who have earned it, not to everyone who enters your energy field. It might seem harsh but it teaches people valuable lessons. If your partner is physically abusive to you giving them respect, adoration and admiration is not going to woo them into offering you the same sort of treatment. Some human beings are just plain a-holes and you are just squandering your precious respect and appreciation by giving it to them. Save it for the worthy ones.

I fully understand all the appreciate your life bumph, loving the precious little flowers and feeling the glow of the glorious burning sun, but you do not have to spend all your time wondering what you can give to someone or a situation. Sometimes, you are doing much more by not giving.

Your aggressive lout of a next door neighbour who plays his music full blast all the time and screams, "Shut up!" to his own baby is not going to become any more agreeable because you offered him a smile. In fact, he is probably going to sneer, "What are you lookin' at?" and punch you in the gob. What he might need instead is a kick up the backside, perhaps in the form of a court order evicting him from the premises. Our reactions have to fit the individual and the circumstances. A smile is not enough to solve everything. It is a tough world and we have to be tough too sometimes.

It has been expressed that abundance is an inner state of being that is then outwardly converted to our own reality. We only get abundance if we have abundance. This of course depends entirely in which context you are using the term 'abundance'. There are hoards of wealthy people who *give* absolutely nothing in terms of money or unconditional love. They might not get any unconditional love back from the Universe or God, when their souls take leave from the earth. However, they do get heaps of terribly expensive 'stuff' and perhaps even love from those around them.

There are some exceedingly spiritual individuals, who consistently follow their higher paths and they do get a lot of unconditional love from the Universe or God, but they are poor in terms of material goods and abused incessantly by other human beings.

People need to be more specific in what they mean by abundance. You will get precisely what you deserve from the Universe, but you might not get what you deserve from other people. This is not the Universe's or God's fault. This is the fault of other humans, who throughout the centuries have exploited spiritually enlightened people. Life is not all happy clappy. Sometimes, it is very tough and we just have to endure it, knowing that something truly beautiful will come out of it. Rather than endure, I should have probably said, accept or perhaps learn, but endure sounded more suitably melodramatic.

In regards to abundance, I have heard a quote from Jesus Christ being used to reinforce the point that abundance derives from our inner state of being. "For to the one who has, more will be given, and from the one who has not, even what he has will be taken away." [2] Just to clarify this, in case there are any ambiguities, this refers to our own connection to the Divine or God. The person, who has a very strong (i.e. abundant) connection to God, will be given much more of God's unconditional love. The person, who has absolutely no connection (i.e. no abundance) to God, will ultimately have all God's unconditional love taken away from them. It might not be in this life, but it will be at their final destination.

So, the moral of the chapter is, if you want to find riches then go for it, but do not trick yourself into believing that it is a spiritual pursuit and do not let money be the driving force in your life. Do what you should be doing and

---

[2] Philippians 4:7 (New Revised Standard Edition.)

if you are meant to have your fortune, it will be so, if you are not, it will not. It is as simple as that really.

There are some exercises coming up that will help you to be accepting of where you are in life and help you to see where the real value lies in this world. They will help you to bestow the most precious thing of all, unconditional love, something that money will never be able to buy.

"Money never made a man happy yet, nor will it. The more a man has, the more he wants. Instead of filling a vacuum, it makes one."

Benjamin Franklin

Techniques

Finding Value

 Grab yourself a piece of paper and a pen and write a list of all the positive aspects of being rich and then a list of all the negative aspects of being rich.

 Put your palms over your eyes and take a slow, deep breath in and out through your nose.

 Take your hands away from your eyes and silently read out the list you have just written.

 Repeat the above two steps, five times.

 Place your left palm over your forehead and your right palm over your navel and take a deep breath in and out through your nose.

 Move your right palm to your heart area and take another deep breath in and out.

 Join your hands in prayer position in front of your chest, with your elbows pointing to the ground.

 Silently say to yourself "May my intuition guide me to see the real value in the world."

Practise this exercise three times a week.

Love Thyself

- ❑ Find a quiet space and sit yourself down, either on a chair or on the floor; keeping your back straight and your palms facing upwards in your lap.

- ❑ Breathe in, slowly through your nose counting to seven. Breathe out through your mouth counting to seven. Repeat this process for between three and ten minutes.

- ❑ Rub your palms together very fast, until they feel hot and then gently place your fingertips over your eyes for a few seconds.

- ❑ Rub your palms together again and gently place them over your mouth.

- ❑ Rub your palms together again and gently place them at either side, over the top of your chest.

- ❑ With your palms still covering the top of your chest, start to breathe in very slowly through your nose and out through your mouth.

- ❑ As you breathe in, visualise a beam of pink light, coming down from far above, entering the top of your head, flowing down your neck and into your chest, where your hands are.

- ❑ As you breathe out, visualise black negative energy pouring up from your chest into your throat and then out of your mouth.

- ❑ Repeat the two steps above for between three and ten minutes.

❑ When you have completed the process, silently say to yourself, "May the Universe turn my negative energy into positive love."

Finding Gratitude

 Grab yourself a piece of paper and a pen and write a list of all the things you feel you have to be grateful for.

 Write another list of the things that you perceive as negative that have happened in your life.

 In a seated position, place your left palm over your heart area and your right palm over your navel and take a slow, deep breath in and out through your nose.

 With your hands still in place, read out the first list and after each item say, "I am truly grateful," then repeat this process with the second list.

 Place your palms at either side, over the top of your chest and repeat the step above.

 Press your left index finger onto the middle of your forehead, between your eyebrows and silently say seven times, "I am truly grateful to the Universe for everything that comes my way. I become more grateful with each new day."

 Join your hands together in prayer position in front of your chest and gently bow forward.

Practise this exercise three times a week.

Good Intentions Are Not Enough...

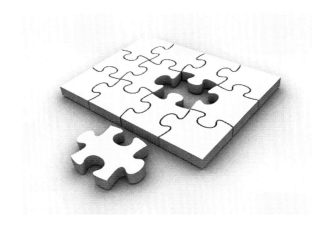

...because they need to be followed with good actions

A Tall Tale

I have to confess, I used to be a bit of a self-help workshop junkie. I headed out to a workshop about three years ago that was all about intention. The gentleman spoke about how the most important thing in life is good intentions. He said that your intention is fundamentally all that counts. I was really so pleased to hear this. I was incredibly worried about my young child being overweight, but eating just made him so happy.

The look on his cherubic little face when he came running in the kitchen to fetch an iced doughnut, melted me every time. His favourite food was hamburgers. After all, life *is* for living, not worrying about every single thing you do. If you worried about everything, you would worry yourself to death. Right?

Just a year later, my beautiful son started developing health problems. He was constantly tired, had constipation, felt thirsty and hungry all the time and was always getting up in the night to go to the toilet. I was completely perplexed and very concerned, so I took him to the doctors.

I sat down in the doctor's surgery and explained my son's symptoms to our GP. He sighed heavily and shook his head. I will never forget what he said to me, "I am going to test your son for diabetes." I was so shocked, how could he have diabetes at such a young age? The tests confirmed the doctor's worst suspicions. My poor boy had type 1 diabetes mellitus.

"How could this possibly have happened?" I said to the doctor, "I love my son." He shook his head again and asked what I had been feeding him, before callously saying, "You are the reason your son has diabetes, madam." I burst into floods of tears. I was so angry with that doctor at first, but when I took my son to see the hospital dietician and after hours researching the importance of good nutrition. I felt ashamed. Sure, my intentions had been quite good. I wanted to keep my son happy, but my actions were awful and my failure to take responsibility lead to his ill health. Thankfully now, his condition is being managed through diet and insulin injections, but I wish I had taken more responsibility in the first place and saved my child from having a needle inserted into his body every single day.

I have learned one very valuable lesson from all this, that good intentions are simply not enough, they have to be followed with good actions. Long gone are the days when I just rested on my good intentions.

Seriously Though...

Good intentions are wonderful. It is fantastic to have good intentions in life. They are a brilliant starting block and you can leap ahead from your good intentions and make powerful moves in life. The problem is that intention is not a solitary concept, it has a best pal and they work really well together. That crucial comrade is called action and good actions should naturally spring from good intentions. If they do not, the good intentions were futile.

Having good intentions without the subsequent good actions is...well, a bit lazy to be honest. It is one big cop out. It means you can have all the good intentions in the world without ever really having to take any responsibility. We can say, "I had the good intention to do one hour of exercise today. I had the intention to start a new healthy lifestyle plan. I had the intention to go to bed early. I had the intention to search for a new job. I had the intention to cut down on my alcohol consumption. I had the intention to quit smoking." And so it goes on and on. We applaud ourselves on our good intentions and settle back down into our cosy little routines, feeling soothed by our well-meaning *intentions*.

Here is the bummer though, those good intentions we had did not matter a jot because we did not do anything about them. The Universe does not think, "Oh well, they had good intentions to live a good life, lets give them a gold star." It is not quite as simple as that. Intention gets lonely without action, they are soul mates. There are many individuals who trudge through life constructing millions of good intentions. They have big plans. Hazard a guess at how many of them actually follow those intentions through? I would guess, not very many, because the world is in a bit of a state and it might not be quite so terrible if everyone followed their good intentions through with good actions.

Intentions that are not followed through may start off on a relatively small scale, but before you know it they creep up on you. Suddenly, the good intentions can become life and death situations. What if a surgeon has the good intention to successfully complete the appendectomy but he got a bit frazzled the night before, had one too many tequilas and now, unfortunately, he had a bit of a blip and his patient popped his clogs? What if the train driver transporting us to work on our regular daily commute smoked a tad too much ganja the night before and he had the well-meaning intention of driving the train correctly, but he missed a signal instead and crashed into another train, injuring and killing some of his own passengers and some of the passengers on the other train to boot?

What if you had the intention to give up smoking, but it did not quite manifest and you developed lung cancer? What if you had the good intention to lead a healthy lifestyle, but you just could not cut down on bad fats and you had a heart attack? What if you had the good intention of keeping your child happy, but you fed them unhealthy foods and they died of a heart attack? What if you spent your entire life having very good intentions, but you never followed through with any of them and it is not until your death bed, when it is too late, that you solemnly wish you had turned those good intentions into actions?

The world is swarming with people with extremely admirable intentions, but for many that is all they are, just intentions. If they never manage to progress any further than that, nothing good will come of it.

However honourable all our intentions might be, we cannot rest on intention alone. What is more, the action that follows has to be exactly the right action to do justice to that good intention. I once had the worthy intention of being very healthy and fit, but in my ignorance, I was sowing the seeds of my own ill health. I foolishly embarked on a protein only diet, whilst exercising six days a week, running for six miles on many of those days and undertaking many other activities.

Our bodies require a good variety of carbohydrates and my lack of carbohydrates caused me an array of health issues. My intentions were quite good, but I was not aware enough to correctly transmute those intentions into positive actions. I was reckless. If you are going to do something you have to do it properly. The intention to do it properly, the intention to be good, the intention to change your life for the better has to translate into the right action to match that intention. Saying, "I am going to eat a healthy diet," and then eating so-called low fat foods that are high in sugar is not a good action, however laudable your initial intention was.

Doctors may have the good intentions of helping patients suffering from depression and anxiety by prescribing them anti-depressants. The reality is that those pills are not dealing with the cause of the problem and a drug is a drug by any other name. World leaders frequently claim to have good intentions, sometimes they may even believe themselves that they have good intentions, but their actions are often quite the opposite. Their intentions may not even really be good intentions to start off with. They just kid themselves that they are. As a species, we excel at self-denial.

If we *are* going to actively pursue our good intentions we need to understand what we are doing. It is no good just steaming in full pelt without knowing precisely what action that intention requires to be classified as a successful and worthy one. We have to do our research. Additionally, saying you have a good intention does not automatically mean that the intention is as you would suggest. For the intention to be good it needs to be born out of intuition and not out of your physical or our emotional desires.

Someone with an eating disorder may think that their intention to deprive themselves of food is a good one, but the rest of society would not perceive it in the same way. A mother may view her intention to spoil her child with gifts and bow to his or her every whim to be a good one, but in reality she is failing to teach the child to have respect and values. Our prime minister may sincerely believe that he has good intentions, but many of the public would disagree. You might believe that your intention to care for your family by running around after them all the time is a good one, but by doing this they may never learn to take responsibility for themselves.

Your interpretation of what a good intention is may not be a truthful and accurate interpretation. The only way it can be truthful and accurate, is if that intention is intuitive. The only way you will know if it is intuitive, is if you have a profound connection with your intuition. The only way that intention can be commuted into a good and accurate action, is if you are aware and intuitive enough to act appropriately.

This is how the process should work, your intuition should guide you into forming a right intention, you should take note of that intention and your physical and emotional bodies should translate that intention into the appropriate action. This is the only way to ensure that your intention is the right one in the first place and that the subsequent action is the correct one to follow that intention. Otherwise, life may carry you off on a journey that you are not too keen on traversing. Life only flows as it should when we intend and act as we should.

Intention to Reality

Intuition

↓

Right intention

↓

Right Action

(.e.g. Intuition - change your diet, Intention - eat more healthily, Action - See a nutritionist and eat genuinely healthy foods.)

I have seen some self-help books and experts claim that your intentions, if you intend strongly enough, can manifest your desires. Well, if what you desire happens to be everything you *need* on a Universal level, then there is some truth in this. Again though, you need to be pro-active and act on those intentions. If you develop cancer and you fully intend to get better, this will aid your recovery, intention is essential, but if you intend to get better and live a detrimental lifestyle that is not conducive to your recovery, you probably will not. Some points need to be laboured and this is one of them. Right action, right action, right action, our intuition thrives on it.

The best thing you can *ever* do is to implicitly trust your intuition, one hundred percent. If you can do this, you will not need to spend *all your time* intending because you will automatically do what you need to do, without any questions. It will happen naturally, as the Universe commands, you will follow the Universe's lead.

When you trust and follow your intuition, everything you need to do in life becomes instinctive, like taking a step, or taking a breath or blinking an eye. You do not think or mull over it for hours, you do not pine and whine for it, you just do it. Your intentions and actions become one, without any hesitation. You think as you should and do as you should and your life flows exactly as it should.

If you keep trying to achieve something and it just will not manifest, perhaps you are not meant to be doing it in the first place. Perhaps, there is another goal you *need* to be aiming for. Ask yourself before you pool all your intention into something, if it is what you are really meant to have. If you resolutely ignore the obstacles that are being placed on your path, you may miss out on a golden opportunity that was genuinely the right one for you. You can only be resolute when your intuition commands it. There is no point in being dogmatic, if it is detrimental to your higher path on earth. Dogmatism is for the enlightened.

> **"We have to exercise wisdom in all that we do and if you try to bend the Universe, it will bend you."**

Intention And The World

My next altercation is with the assertions of some self-help experts that you can change the world with intention. I have heard it said that we have a Divine gift, which bestows us with the ability to heal the entire world. Once we all realise that we possess this amazing gift, we will be able to prevent and halt catastrophic environmental disasters.

The world is a very big place, inhabited by billions of individuals. You can help some individuals. You can help the people whom you are destined to help, the ones that cross your path for that very reason. But, you **cannot** change the whole world. If something is meant to happen, it will most definitely happen, in spite of your best intentions. No one human being is God. An individual or group cannot tamper with the laws of the Universe.

I hate to be the one to break it to you, but you cannot change the weather by willing it to do so and you cannot allay natural disasters. You are not that powerful and I am not that powerful.

As human beings we sometimes like to think that we have this astonishing amount of control, but we have to learn, that we have so very little. We need to stop trying to control the Universe, because it can shake this fragile earth to its very foundations and we would be destroyed in a flash. Trying to dominate the Universe lacks humility and insight. I often think that we are blind to our own vulnerability and in egotism we believe that we can manifest anything we choose. Not only this, but we feel that we know the best possible outcome.

We can only manifest what we are allowed to choose and we are rarely enlightened enough to understand the full implications of our situations.

This planet is in its current predicament because of our actions and our best intentions will never be enough to change that, unless they are accompanied by the appropriate actions.

Sending your well-meaning intentions or prayers to the victims of Tsunami will not change their lives. Sending your intentions or prayers to starving people in third-world countries will not change their lives. Sending intentions or prayers, or healing, or your love, to bring peace to the world will not change the world. Only when all world governments get up off their backsides and make positive changes, will this world change for the better. Your intentions and energies would be better served helping those around you, that you are able to help and intrinsically, helping yourself.

You can make small steps. There are things that you can do to make a difference. For instance, you could semi-opt out of society by becoming a freegan. You could express your dissatisfaction about the poor treatment of animals by becoming a Vegan. You could avoid the consumption of GM food and pesticides by going all-organic. You could avoid personally contributing to global warming by living a more ecological lifestyle.

Of course there are things *you can do*, but for one, all these things require action and secondly, you can only make inroads on a very limited scale. Do not waste your time and previous energy sending your intentions to world events or catastrophes that you cannot change.

If you want to help the victims of Tsunami, get a job with Christian Aid and go out there and physically help them. There are people who do wonderful work in these kinds of fields. If you want to minimise your contribution to global warming, use your car less often or buy an electric car and modify your home and lifestyle accordingly. Driving your car more frequently, pumping out emissions and intending for the world to be saved, is futile. Do not waste your time that could be used elsewhere sending your good intentions. It is yet another cop out, the lazy person's way. For the world to become a better place, every single one of us needs to take positive action, but the reality is that not every single one of us will. I will discuss these concepts further in a later chapter.

I know this all sounds disheartening, but remember that we all have a purpose, there are things we all need to and should be doing. You are best serving yourself and others by concentrating on these areas, rather than the ones where you cannot make any difference. By focusing on these areas, you can become truly happy and you can make a *real* difference to the people that require *your* assistance. Also, remember that intentions require good actions. If you can let your intuition always be your guide and allow your intentions and actions to naturally follow, you will be well on the way to living a more contented and worthwhile life.

The exercises at the end of this chapter will, as in the other chapters, help you to better trust your own intuition, the most important step we can all take in life. They will also help you to take a look at your own life and see where you can turn your good intentions into good actions. This way you can make a genuine difference to your own life and help others in the right way for them.

"The evil that is in the world almost always comes of ignorance, and good intentions may do as much harm as malevolence if they lack understanding."

Albert Camus

Ten Things You Cannot Do With Intention

1. Bend the will of the Universe.

2. Change the laws of the Universe.

3. Change the course of the Universe.

4. Bring about world peace.

5. Heal the world.

6. Prevent natural castastrophes.

7. Win the Lottery.

8. Make someone love you.

9. Make changes that require actual actions.

10. Prevent anyone's time to die.

Techniques

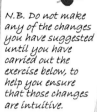

What can I change?

Write a list of all the areas in your life where you can make constructive changes. For each item add your intention and suggested actions to achieve each change.

N.B. Do not make any of the changes you have suggested until you have carried out the exercise below, to help you ensure that those changes are intuitive.

Intuitive Insight

❏ Grab the list you made for the exercise above.

❏ Sit down comfortably with your back straight, either on the floor or in a chair. Place the list in your lap.

❏ Silently read your list out to yourself, including all the intentions and suggested actions.

❏ After you have finished reading your list, blink five times.

❏ Repeat the above two steps five times.

❏ Join your hands in prayer position in front of your chest. Start to breathe in and out through your nose very slowly and focus your attention on the feeling of your palms touching each other. Carry out this process for between three and five minutes.

❏ Place your palms over the list and silently say to yourself with meaning and purpose, five times, "May the Universe guide me to intuitively see, what constructive changes I can make in my life to become the real Divine me."

❑ Put your hands back in prayer position and gently bow.

Find somewhere prominent in your home, like a pin board or on the fridge, to pin up your list and over the next couple of months you should intuitively receive the guidance you have requested. On receiving the guidance, draw a star by the change you are intending to initiate and set about making that change. Allow your intuition to guide you and be accepting of what comes your way, whether you perceive it as good or bad.

Accepting What I Cannot Change?

 Grab yourself a piece of paper and a pen and write down a list of things that you cannot change in life.

 Place your left palm over the middle of your forehead with your fingers pointing upwards and place your right palm over your list.

 With you hands still in place, silently say to yourself seven times, "I accept what I cannot change, I bow to the will of the Universe. I live for my path on earth and accept what my path has in store."

 Place your palms over your eyes for a few seconds, then over your cheeks and finally on either side of your navel for a few seconds.

Practise this exercise a few times a week.

You Cannot Have, Be, Or Do, Anything You Desire...

...because it may not be within Universal will

A Tall Tale

I always wanted to be a runner. I used to dream about it as a child. The problem was, I was absolutely useless at running. We had competitions at school and I was always the one that finished last. On one school sports day, I took part in a one-hundred-metre sprint. I eagerly took off along with the other kids, but in all my enthusiasm I lost one of my trainers. I was so perplexed. I did not know whether to rescue my shoe or just continue with the race. Everyone had a good old chuckle at my expense and by the time I had decided what to do about my shoe, the race was already over.

Despite that, I never gave up. I even became pretty good at it. Yet, no matter how damn hard I tried, there were always people that dashed past me without even breaking out into a sweat. Still, I was not put off by these minor obstacles and I joined a county athletics group. I had improved vastly with practise and I had visions of being a top athlete.

On my first run with the running group, I nearly got lost. The entire group went shooting off ahead and I think they got so bored of waiting for me, in the end that they gave up! Still, I began to focus all my intention on my running. I had a part-time job but that was just bread and butter. I was doggedly focused on my main goal. Running was my passion and nothing was going to stand in my way, no obstacle, big or small.

On one of my usual runs, I noticed that I was feeling very tired and losing my concentration. I felt a twang in my left leg and as I looked down to survey the afflicted area, I lost my balance and tumbled onto my leg. I let out a rip-roaring scream. I have never felt pain like it, before or since that event. I sat there for a couple of minutes clutching my leg before a lady came past and telephoned for an ambulance for me.

The prognosis was not good. I had fractured my left leg and the doctor said I would need a metal plate. She also informed me that I should give up my running because on scanning my back, they had discovered a degenerative spine condition that would be exacerbated by running or jogging. I was devastated. If I could not run, what could I do?

Months later, after spending hours moping around the house feeling sorry for myself, I realised something. I was never meant to be a runner. No matter how hard I tried, it did not come naturally to me. It became apparent to me that by pooling all my efforts into this one area, I had neglected my other talents. Just because I wanted it so badly, it did not mean that it was the right thing for me.

As my leg got better and I took steps to help my back condition, I began to stop trying to control my path. I made a vow to myself and the Universe that I would accept what I was here to do. It was such a relief to have that acceptance. It was such a relief to relinquish my vain attempts to control everything.

Strangely enough, a few weeks later I was reading the employment section in the local newspaper, not particularly expecting to find anything and I noticed a job that interested me. I applied for it without really thinking about it. I did not expect to hear anything back, but I did. I got an interview a week later and then they called me and told me I had the job a week after that. I could not believe it. Part of me wishes that I had not wasted so much time focusing my attention on the wrong areas, but I have learned a good lesson from it, you cannot have, be or do anything you want in life because it may never have been meant for you.

Seriously Though...

Usually I am not one to quote music artists. It is a tad tacky, but the Rolling Stones put it so *terribly* well, "You can't always get what you want, but if you try sometimes you just might find you get what you need." In fact, if what you want is totally out of line with what the Universe thinks you should be getting, you will be lucky to get anything you want at all. If you constantly obsess over your desires and beg the Universe to realise them, the Universe might say, "Well ok then, you can have what you asked for, but there will be a price to pay later on." Of course, you may not hear the Universe saying this, but everything has a price in life. We should be careful what we wish for.

Some highly-praised self-help literature presents the argument that we are here on this earth to fulfil our desires, that our intentions and thoughts create our own reality. We choose our reality and that reality depends on what thoughts we are manifesting. Like attracts like, right? Some people merrily instruct the Universe to give them exactly what they want. Apparently, the Law of Attraction produces whatever our minds conjure. If you have positive thoughts, you will attract positive energy your way and if you have negative thoughts, you will attract negative energy to you.

There is an element of truth in this. I do believe that our thoughts are really energy. If we constantly have negative thoughts about ourselves and other people, we almost evoke a negative energy that could potentially be detrimental. Many of us have heard somewhere along the line about the power of creative visualisation. Some people with life threatening illnesses have used positive thoughts to improve their health. If you tell yourself, "That is it, I am going to die, I give up," you are telling your body to do precisely that. So, I applaud generating positive thoughts. You can make your life better by being a more positive person.

The thing is, and you might see this as a dampener, but just because you desire something really badly, it does not guarantee that you will get what you want. Telling God to provide you with a Mercedes or informing the Universe that you would like a swish new pad in the Maldives, is not going to guarantee you the outcome you desire. You can mull over it all day long and say, "I am going to be a CEO and get my comfy, opulent house, I am, I am, I am. I can already see it in my head. I am a CEO of a big corporation. I am manifesting my desire. I am breaking through all obstacles. Nothing will stand in my way."

If it is within your path on earth, you may be given what you have asked for, but if it is not, all your visualisation and intention will mean jack. So, in all honesty, we cannot have, be and do as we please, we can only have, be and do what the Universe *allows* us to do. Moreover, what makes us think we are entitled to these things? We need to accept what the Universe gives us rather than asking for stuff we are not entitled to. Just because we want something, it does not mean that firstly, we should get it and secondly, that it will make us happy. In fact, there are many people who get what they ask for and it makes them utterly miserable.

We do have choices, to a degree, but not an infinite amount of choices. I believe it is highly arrogant to think that we can entirely construct our own reality. We can create it to a degree, but the Universe can snap it up faster than you can yell "Yee-haa." What the Universe gives, the Universe can just as easily take away. What you want on the grand scale of things means relatively little, unless what you want happens to be what you need.

The best way to lead a fulfilling and truly happy life is to learn to want what you need, rather than chasing desires that will never be yours. And before you all start saying, "But what about all the people who have achieved their dreams, who read all the self-help books and went for their goals and realised them..." etc etc. That is their path. It does not mean that it is yours. I am not claiming that you can never achieve any of your goals, but what I am saying is that you can only achieve the goals that are within the remit of your path on earth.

If you can come to want what you need in life, you can achieve all of your goals, because your new goals will automatically be in line with the will of the Universe. If you can dare to surrender some of your more physical desires and follow your intuition, you may in good time, be given some of them back. You will also be a lot happier because we can only ever be truly happy when we fulfil our true purposes for being here.

If you blithely storm through life in pursuit of your physical and emotional desires without taking heed of what you really need, you will never understand the meaning of completeness or being at peace. Peace comes from letting go, to something far greater than we are. Whether you call that something God, the Universe, destiny, Spirit, the Source, is irrelevant. It is what it is, regardless of how we construe it and when we succumb to it, we become much better and happier individuals. We come to Life.

Without banging on about myself too much, because I do not want to bore you to death, I am going to cite what happened to me as an example of how bowing to the will of the Universe can change your life for the better.

When I was younger I had many dreams. For a while, I wanted to a fashion designer, then a pop star (well I was only three), then a graphic designer, then a journalist, then an author and so on. My real passion was for anything creative. Like so many other people, I went to school and got some qualifications. Then I went to university and did a degree in politics. I wished afterwards that I had studied graphic design instead. I got temporary employment in an administration role and found it distinctly lacklustre. I could not figure out how some people could go through life plodding the same old routine, doing their nine to five, living for the weekend and accepting their lot. I really wanted to work in advertising, so I applied for some jobs but I never got anywhere.

To cut a long and very dull story short, I developed a bad back condition and after a range of conventional and unconventional treatments had made no difference, I went to see a Reiki practitioner. Someone at work had happened to mention Reiki, so I thought I would give it a go. It helped a bit, so I thought, "Why not go on a Reiki course," and so that is exactly what I did. So, without any real expectations I went to the Reiki course and it changed my entire life in one day. I had to self-heal every day with Reiki, which I did for hours because I enjoyed it so much. There was personal effort involved, but there always is in anything worthwhile.

Over three years I discovered my true purpose for being on earth, I found a partner, I gained self-esteem from being my true higher self. I gained immense knowledge of the Universe, my place in the Universe and so much more. I gave up some pastimes I had previously enjoyed including: running, which was damaging my back, drinking alcohol, eating meat and chocolates and sweets and going to pubs and clubs. I self-healed with Reiki everyday. I also gave up on my former dream of being in advertising and put my creativity aside to focus on treating people with Reiki and teaching Reiki courses.

None of this felt at all like a sacrifice. I felt so much happier and lighter and I still do. I did not try to control the Universe, I became guided by the Universe and did what the Universe and my intuition guided me to do. I accepted that everything in my life was a blessing, whether painful or pleasant. I learned to want what I needed.

When I had done all of this, some dreams I had put to the back of my mind started popping to the fore. I quickly became a journalist, then shortly after, I became a features editor of a women's lifestyle magazine. I wrote a book. I wanted to design my business website, so I taught myself how to do it. I then ended up designing a couple of other websites. I wrote another book. Then I became an eco-stylist, styling people with ethical fashion items. Although I had to put the hard work, effort and hours in, it did not feel like a chore because I thoroughly enjoyed what I was doing. Effort only seems like an effort when you are discontent with what you are doing.

I love the way my life has changed. I love being me and the journey I am on. I am so grateful for everything and I become more grateful with each new day. So in all of my warbling, the point I am trying to make is that, I let go. I let go of what I had wanted in life. I made a pact with the Universe that I would follow my path, that I would follow its will and not my own. When I finally let go, I was given some of my lifelong dreams and they meant so much more to me, because this time, I felt I really deserved them and they were not just about me, but about helping others find their path.

So, if you follow your path, if you trust and follow your intuition, if you let go and allow the Universe to be your ultimate guide, you may be given what you want, but only when you have earned it.

Not everyone can be an Olympic athlete, a company director, a CEO, a movie star, a pop star, a catwalk model, a life coach, a personal trainer, a celebrity stylist, a footballer, or whatever the occupation may be. Many people now are looking for fame for fame's sake, for adulation and glory. People are very often desperate for recognition from others, but this kind of recognition is temporal. We should not *need* recognition from any one person on this earth, but from our intuition and from the Universe, or if you prefer, God. If you have a personal dream, you have to ask yourself why you are so keen to achieve it. Why do you want that dream job? Is there something else that would be more suitable for your path and for you? What would really make you happy? Forget for a second about the money, status and power that that dream brings. Real power comes from being connected with your intuition, from trusting in your higher path, from being your true self. This is what really empowers us, being true to ourselves.

Living life is not about the stories you are going to tell your grandchildren, it is not about what you leave behind. Life is about what you learned, how you developed yourself spiritually, how you evolved as a soul. When you die, you cannot take your worldly dreams with you. You cannot take your possessions with you, or your job title, or the adulation and recognition of the people around you. Even if you do not believe in life after death, if you believe that this life here is all we have. When your body is decomposing in its coffin, what will any of the physical goals you once achieved mean? Nothing.

I personally do not believe that anyone, if they are truly honest with themselves, only believes in this one life here on earth. If you do, you have to ask yourself, what is the point of anything? Why be good or bad, why do anything at all? You wonder if there is more to life because there is. You do not have to believe in God or religion, just to have faith in your intuition.

We all **know** the truth, if we would be brave enough to accept it. If you believe that life is just about making it what we want it to be, then go for your goals and see where it takes you, but always be prepared to accept the consequences of your actions. If you attain your goals and still do not feel happy and complete, then ask yourself why? Sometimes, we achieve something we think will make us happy but when we make it past the finish line, it no longer seems like such a triumph. We shift the goal posts and broaden our goals, but the reality is often quite different from the dream, unless the dream happens to be, the Way of the Universe.

A Price To Pay

More than ever, I think that people see what society would deem as high achievers or successful individuals around them and they aspire to be exactly like them. They see what those successful people have, they see how happy they look and they want a portion of the pie. They think, "Why shouldn't I have some of that happiness, wealth and success? Why should I settle for my lot?"

Well, first of all, no one is asking anyone to settle for their lot. We can all be happy, as I have said before, if we trust in and follow our intuition. As we endeavour to do this, life flows as it should and we become more accepting and grateful. Secondly, just because someone appears to have everything, it does not mean that they actually do. The real wealth of the world is spiritual wealth and if we lack that, we lack everything, our souls live in poverty.

People can appear to be content, they can present a facade. Sometimes, they may even convince themselves they are happy when they are truly not. You can convince yourself of anything if you try hard enough. All physical happiness is ephemeral. Real happiness is eternal and how many people do you know who have that?

Try to look beyond the images that people portray to others. We are an exceedingly proud species and we do not like others to observe our vulnerabilities. You might think that some people have perfect lives, but the chances are that the reality does not quite match the impeccable picture they paint.

In the chapter on fear, I talked about consequences. If you remember, I gave some examples of the consequences of certain occupations in life. Whatever you choose to do in life there will be a consequence for you and for others. If you are resolute on doing it, that is your choice, but be prepared to accept those consequences.

We often hear pop stars and celebrities moaning about media intrusion and how they feel that they can never have a moment to themselves. If you want to go into that industry, if you want fame; that is the price you have to pay. If you do not like that price then find another dream, one that will work for you.

Wanting something badly, is not enough, it has to be within your destiny. If it is not, tough luck, utilise your other talents. There are people in the world dying and starving, who wonder every day if that day will be their last. Their dreams are probably quite simple: to have more food, clean water and a roof over their heads. There are many people living in war torn countries who hear bombs flying over their houses every single day, who never know if there will be an end to the fighting. Some of them will have never known what it feels like to not live in perpetual fear. In the Western World we are lucky, we have more opportunities and choices than we often realise. We need to learn to be wiser with our dreams and choices.

For everything in life, there is a price to pay. You do not get anything for free. For everything you take from life, things will be taken away from you. For everything you earnestly and intuitively give to life, things will be bestowed upon you, but they might not be what you had expected. For every single thought or action there is a consequence.

The Universe once existed in perfect balance, but we are tipping the scales. There are more and more people who are taking from the Universe, recklessly abusing the Universe and failing to take responsibility for their lives. There are less people giving their unconditional love, acting honestly and living their lives in a conscious way. In the Western world we have become accustomed to a particular way of life and we want to have certain things at any cost. If we do not have them we feel inadequate, frustrated and agitated, but we have to ask ourselves in earnest, are some of those things really worth having?

We should not be competing with other people, worrying about what they do or do not have, obsessing about our physical and material goals, living fecklessly and trying to make the Universe give us what we want to have and damn the consequences. We need to worry less about what others have, about what our society perceives as being the route to success and material wealth. We need to worry more about how consciously we are living our lives, what we are doing for the Universe and what we are doing for the good of our true higher selves.

We live very separate lives, but are we really separate? I personally, do not think so. Humans are all part of the same energy and every single thing we do affects the balance of the Universe for good or for bad and for better or for worse. Everyone has to make sacrifices to be where they want to be in life. Before we steam in, chasing what we think are our dreams, we need to ask ourselves if the outcome is worth the endeavour.

Positive thoughts are great and those thoughts need to lead to positive action, but we need to be intuitive enough to perceive what a positive thought is. We need to intuitively understand if our dreams are positive and part of our path. Above all, we need to let go to the will of the Universe and let that always, be our greatest guide.

The exercises at the end of this chapter will help you to be more accepting of what comes your way and to let go and be guided. If you can achieve this, you will hopefully be pleasantly surprised at what comes your way. It might not be what you had expected, but it will be welcome.

"Do not spoil what you have by desiring what you have not; remember that what you now have was once among the things you only hoped for."

Epicurus

Techniques

Letting Go

 Grab yourself a piece of paper and a pen and write a list of all your dreams and aspirations.

 Sit down comfortably, with your back straight, either on a chair or on the floor.

 Read your dreams out loud one by one and then turn the piece of paper face down on the floor.

 Join your hands in prayer position in front of your chest and take five deep breaths in and out through your nose.

 Visualise a white beam of light coming down from as far up above as the eye can see and entering the top of you head. Allow the light beam to morph into a ball of light, inside your head, covering your entire brain.

 Say out loud seven times, "I present my dreams and wishes to the Universe, I let go of them completely to follow my path."

 Repeat the above three steps, three times.

 When you have finished bow and then pat the top of your head three times with your left hand.

Practise this exercise four times a week.

Positive Acceptance

❑ Lie down comfortably on the floor; with your arms resting by your sides and your palms facing upwards.

❑ Breathe in and out very slowly through your nose, as you gently wiggle your fingers. Breathe in, for a count of five and out for a count of five. Continue with this process for between one and three minutes.

❑ Take a deep breath in through your nose, until your lungs feel completely full and then let out a giant sigh, coming right from your diaphragm. Repeat this three times.

❑ Place your left palm on your heart area, in the middle of your breastbone and your right palm over your navel area.

❑ Take a deep breath in and then another giant sigh.

❑ Visualise a huge beam of green light coming from up above, as far as the eye can see and entering your entire body from top to toe. For a few moments or minutes, remain completely focused on your body being engulfed in the light.

❑ Silently say to yourself, with meaning and purpose, fifteen times, "I accept whatever life throws my way, I accept my purpose and live with love for each new day."

❑ Take a deep breath in, release one more giant sigh and as you do so, visualise black negative liquid pouring out of your mouth. See that black energy leave your body and the room completely.

❑ Silently say, "May the Universe turn this negative energy into positive light."

❑ Return your palms to the floor facing upwards and relax for a few moments to finish the technique.

Motives

 Keep a note pad and a pen by your bed and every morning when you first wake, ask yourself, "What is my main motivation in life?" Write down the first thing that pops into your weary head.

 Each night before you go bed silently say, "May the Universe guide me to see what should be my motivation. May the Universe guide me to see the real me." Continue by asking the Universe to show you the answers in your dreams.

 Every morning when you wake up, write down the dreams you can remember, before writing your motivations in life.

 Following this silently say to yourself, "May the answers in my dreams translate into my life. May the path I follow be what my dreams have described."

 Continue with this for a month and notice how different your motivations become in that time. Once you feel that your motivations are truly intuitive you can stop and begin to act on that intuition . Otherwise, continue until you reach this point. You might be very surprised by what comes to you.

Remember to LET GO. Allow the will of the universe to dictate the flow of your life. BE HONEST with yourself. Don't pin all your hopes on one dream. BE OPEN to other options. BE GUIDED by your intuition.

"I feel there are two people inside me – me and my intuition. If I go against her, she'll screw me every time, and if I follow her, we get along quite nicely."

Kim Basinger

Do Not Look For Good In Everyone...

...because it will distract you from your own purpose

A Tall Tale

I used to think that there was good in every single person. In my personal life, I always seemed to get drawn to a certain sort of man, the ones that made it particularly difficult to see *any* good in them, let alone *some* good. My family would say, "Why don't you leave him?" but I felt that everyone, in their heart of hearts had an inner spark of goodness. I thought that if I looked and tried hard enough, I could turn that spark into a flame.

I had watched a television programme that said we should try hard to look beyond the surface and discover the inner beauty that resided within each and every one of us. I thought with each of my partners, with everyone in fact, that there was something worth fighting for, so no matter how much I got hurt I never once gave up.

I distinctly remember the turning point. I was with this particular beau who was so angry all the time. He never once had anything nice to say about anyone and he certainly had nothing nice to say about me. I always used to give him the benefit of the doubt. My friends would say, "Why are you wasting your time with that idiot?" I would then defend him and say things like, "Well at least he does some nice things, like cook me breakfast and occasionally he buys me flowers and after we argue and fight, he is always so apologetic."

I woke up next to him and watched him, as he slept. I started to think about all the things he had done to me. He had been so abusive and aggressive, pushing me around and sometimes throwing plates and my ornaments at me. I lost count of how many of my favourite ornaments he smashed. He was constantly putting me down. I was starting to feel so low that I ended believing what he was saying. I believed that I was stupid and pathetic and worthless.

As I thought about all these things, I began to ponder on my other relationships. It dawned on me that my life had followed this terrible vicious cycle and not once had I tried to break free from it. I almost thrived on being with people who were aggressive and hostile. I thought I could save them. As these thoughts whirred around in my mind, I thought about how my life could have been so different. I had never lived for myself because I was always living to help someone else.

I looked down at him, really intently. He opened his eyes and said, "What are you looking at?" In that moment, I saw it. I saw nothing, no light, no spark of inner beauty, no joy, no love and no light. It occurred to me then that this man, all these men I had been in relationships with, all the aggressive people I had wasted my time around, they had distracted me from my own happiness. They had veered me off my path in life. Then I thought, you can find good where there is good to find, but sometimes, no matter how hard you look for it, the good is not there.

After that, my life changed. I took the opportunity to get in touch with my own intuition, with my own true self. I found out who I really was and I found my path in life. I steered well clear of people who could possibly draw me away from my path.

I came to believe that there is good in a lot of people, but sometimes if you spend too much time looking for good, you come to ignore the bad and you realise the life you lived was never for you. So my advice to anyone would be, do not look for good in everyone, because it will distract you from your own purpose in life.

Seriously Though...

I would like to postulate that there is **not** good to be found
in everyone. I do not believe that deep down, everyone, is
fundamentally a good person. This may not make me terribly
popular with some psychologists and self-help experts, but it
is my opinion. Some people are good. Some people behave
really quite atrociously, but there is good in them somewhere
and at some point it may unravel, or it may not. Some people
are not good at all. They seek to afflict pain on others. They
never give consideration to the consequences of their actions
and they will, thus, never become better people. They will
never even desire to. It is not enough to state that all people

who behave badly are just frightened individuals behaving in harmful or evil ways. Letting people off the hook and putting it down to fear is not a good way to help them or you.

It is not quite a case of the good, the bad and the ugly but the concept is getting there. We do not have to try and see the good in everyone. For our own personal growth and well-being, we should be avoiding the people that waste our time and energy. We need to understand that not everyone can become a good person. First of all, not everyone wants to do the right thing and what is more, some people are not meant to do the right thing. They are here to do the exact opposite, which whilst it might not be right in our eyes, is their task on a Universal level.

Why should we expend our very precious time and energy on trying to help people who cannot and do not want to be helped? I suggest that we should help the people we can help, be around the people that are conducive to our personal and spiritual growth and to hell with the rest. Why give someone the time of day that only seeks to draw you down to their level? If you cannot raise them up to yours, then why bother trying? Some people thrive off making other people suffer. Why should we try and see a Divine spark in them? I posit that if you cannot see it intuitively, then it is not there.

I do not think the world would be in quite such as state, if there were genuine good in every person. I am sure you can think of certain people that you have come across in your life and regardless of what they said to you and how charmingly they conveyed their message, you had this little niggling intuition, a bit of the heebie geebies, that, "urgh go away" feeling. You may well have given them the benefit of the doubt, but deep down in the pit of your stomach you felt a distinct sense of uneasiness, like there was something quite unnerving and sinister about them. That marked uneasiness you felt was your intuition throwing out a beacon saying, "Beware, beware bad person alert. Stay away." Why did your intuition want you to stay away? Because they would cause you some form of harm if you did not. It may not necessarily be physical harm, but potentially it could be. What is more, they would have taken delicious pleasure in drawing you away from your purpose in life, because if they can make you unhappy it will serve their own purpose.

The problem is we like to try and see the good in all people. For some reason, it temporarily soothes us. There was a time when I used to try and see the good in *all* people. It was in between the loathing all people and realising that only some people are good phase that I am now in. It was when I first learned Reiki. I wanted to share it with the whole planet. I wanted to heal everyone and make the entire world a better place. I thought it was a lovely notion that the whole world could possibly be made a better place. How funny and fantastical that seems in retrospect. I found it all somewhat perplexing when I discovered that not everyone wanted my help. It was not long before I realised four significant things.

The first realisation was that there were some really good individuals on the planet who allowed right thinking and right living to pervade every area of their lives, whatever walk of life they happened to be in. These people would always be good people and even if they temporarily stumbled off their path, they would find their way back onto it again. These people could be helped.

The second realisation was that there were some OK people on the planet, who kind of meandered through life and did not take a whole lot of responsibility for themselves.

They spent much of their life on their physical paths and at some point they might have taken a step over and embraced their spiritual paths as well.

The third realisation was that there were a significant number of altogether unpleasant people on the planet, but this unpleasantness was partly a product of their upbringing. If they were presented with a different way of living, if they were given the choice they might take it. On the other hand they might not and if they were not prepared to take the choice, there was no point wasting any time on them.

The fourth realisation was that there were people who were just intrinsically bad and no amount of cajoling was going to make them otherwise. These people were just best avoided at any cost. They could be in any walk of life. They could be a barrister, a judge, a manager at work, a street sweeper, a care taker, a politician, a circus performer, anyone really. The chances were though, that many of them would try to get in a position of power where they could readily take advantage of the vulnerable.

Think of all the positions of power where vulnerable people can be exploited. People can be hugely exploitative in any industry, but bad people want to be in a prime position to take full advantage. They could be doctors or teachers, complementary therapists, preachers or even world leaders. I am sure you could write down a list of suspects now, we see some of them splashed over the national newspapers and television screens.

Of course, good and bad on a Universal level do not have quite the same connotations. Everyone has a purpose whether we view that purpose as good or bad. Good and bad is a terribly human concept, but if we view someone as bad, why should we be around them or give them credit where no credit is due? I do not believe that we should. They may have a purpose but it does not mean that they can tear us away from ours.

With all that said, helping others can be remarkably rewarding. The thing is to know whom you can and cannot help. If we try to help people who cannot be helped, they will draw us away from our own self-development and not only that, they will pull us away from those who genuinely need our help.

People get stuck in all sorts of unhealthy relationships with others, where they deeply want to make a difference and their failure is not from lack of trying. If this is you, if you are around someone in whatever context that you have devoted so much time to helping, but you have received nothing in return, it's time to ask yourself, "Can I really help this person or am I completely wasting my time?" If the answer is the latter, then it is vital that you re-evaluate your relationships. You are so much better than that. Don't let anyone drag you down. Focus on **your** path. Focus on finding your intuitive self. Trust in what you know. Just because someone declares to you that they are wise, or intelligent, or a good person, it does not mean that they truthfully are. You know better than that.

You know the truth, if you look hard enough inside of you. You may be saying, "Yeah, yeah, I have heard it all before. This is all just common sense." There is a great deal of wisdom in common sense. Unfortunately, too few people rely on it. They rely on others and right now someone who does not deserve your time could be relying on you. If they are, if they are taking you away from your intuitive guidance, then maybe it is time to do something about it.

Four Types of People

1. Really good people who lead really good lives most of the time. Can be helped.

2. Ok people that sometimes lead good lives and sometimes do not. Can be helped in some cases.

3. Not so good people that have done a lot of bad things. Can be helped in some cases.

4. Bad people that never lead good lives. Cannot be and do not want to be helped.

Knowing How To Help

Once you have established whether you can help someone or not, it is important to know how to help them in the most appropriate manner. Just because we *believe* we are helping someone, it does not mean that we actually *are*. I know I keep labouring the point about intuition, but if we cannot trust in our intuition we cannot truly know how to help someone effectively.

There is helping on a superficial level and helping on an intuitive level. Sometimes, what we perceive as helping someone actually pulls us away from our own purpose and does not help the person we are trying to assist at all. Helping is not merely about physically doing something for people, sometimes it involves standing back from situations, telling someone some harsh home truths and sometimes it means doing nothing at all.

We often get too emotionally entangled in situations and far too attached. To offer help to anyone in an effective way we need to be healthily detached. By being detached we can offer our help in a more objective way. Being detached means we can care without really caring. This way we can offer help without allowing our own emotions to become emotionally embroiled with other peoples' problems.

As a personal example, in my Reiki practice people come to me with a wide variety of physical and emotional issues. With each client I am empathetic, understanding and I carefully listen to what they have to say. I do not give direct advice, in other words I do not tell people exactly what to do in their lives. That is their choice and not mine. I do however offer general objective guidance. I always base that guidance on intuition, regardless of my own personal experiences or bias. I try to look at all sides of the situation.

When the client leaves, I forget all about their issues and problems. I no longer care what they do because it is entirely up to them. I do not get bogged down with everyone else's emotional issues. If I did, I would not be a very good practitioner or teacher because my objectivity and ability to see beyond what the client presents to me would be entirely compromised.

Being objective and detached is easier with strangers than it is with family, friends and other loved ones. However, having said that, as your intuition develops you become more detached with loved ones as well. This does not equate to not loving them, but to loving them in a much healthier and if you like, in a more Divine way. By doing this, you are able to help them in a more productive manner because rather than offering subjective suggestions that may not be in their best interests, you will always offer objective guidance.

Subjective advice is not only detrimental to those around you, but to yourself because, by being so wrapped up in someone else's problems you can end up neglecting areas of your own life and path on earth that desperately require your attention.

The assistance we offer to any individual should be beneficial to their soul path above and beyond all else. You might sometimes have to give some harsh home truths and it might cause some upset to the individual you are trying to help. However, if the truth means that the individual will do the right thing and it will help them to grow spiritually, then telling the truth is worth doing.

We have to be so intuitive about the advice we give. If, for example you have a friend with children, who smokes cigarettes and it is making them ill, you could just let them carry on, or say something vague like, "Are you sure you should be smoking in your condition. Maybe you should give it up?" Alternatively, intuition permitting, you could instead say something a bit more coarse like, "If you do not stop smoking it could kill you one day and if it does not kill you, it will kill your children." You are not telling them what to do, but you are making them aware of the consequences of their actions. This is incredibly important. If someone is ignoring the consequences of their actions, or is not aware of the consequences, we sometimes need to make them aware, to furnish them with a choice. Ignorance deprives us of choices, but awareness bestows us with choices. Then it is up to us whether we make those choices or not.

We have a tendency to be namby pamby, politically correct and wishy-washy in the Western world, but some people need an ample dose of tough love. You might be doing someone more harm than good by just watching them continue with the same destructive patterns of behaviour and saying absolutely nothing.

It is worth noting, that whilst we can help someone know their choice, we cannot take that choice away from them. In some cases we have to stand back and do nothing. People have to make choices for the right reasons, because they want to do the right thing. You can tell someone some home truths, but after that, it is up to them to make the choices they need to make. You can tell someone about the dangers of smoking and try to offer a bit of help, but if they still want to carry on doing it despite the consequences that is their choice.

If your best friend is on a diet that is damaging her, and you can see that she is becoming thin and withdrawn, you can perhaps say, "You know you can always come to me if you want to talk about anything." You can provide general guidance and a listening ear. If necessary, you can refer them to specialist help and get some professionals involved, but if she is not prepared to change, there is nothing you can do. Again, you can offer general advice.

It is always hard to watch people we love damaging themselves, but there is only so much we can do. We cannot and should not force our help onto anyone. People need to do the right things for the right reasons. If we take their choice away, they will end up being given the same lessons over and over again until they choose to do the right things for the right reasons. Maybe they never will and that is a hard pill to swallow, but we have to swallow it none the less.

Obviously, we have to exercise common sense at all times. If someone is in a life or death situation, if someone is being physically abused, if someone is breaking the law, we might have to get professionals or even the law involved in some cases. Once we have done this, we have to take a step back and let the professionals or law perform their duties.

Trying to see the good in everyone is a waste of time, in my honest opinion. We would be better serving ourselves and other people by looking for the good in those where it is present and then we can get on with serving our own paths on earth. Intuitively, we all have the ability to weigh people up and we **can** help some people. In fact, when we do help people in the right way for their path, it enriches our lives and it enriches their lives, but we cannot help everyone and we cannot look for good in everyone. Sometimes, it is as plain as day that the good is absent and when it is, we should make a sharp exit.

The exercises at the end of this chapter will help you to see people as they really are. Some people try to trick our intuition with cunning words and body language, but our intuition is no fool. If we capitalise on our latent abilities to sniff out the truth, we can offer help to those who need it, we can help ourselves to become better people and the rest can do as they wish, but always knowing the consequences.

Jesus said: "The wise person is perfect in all wisdom, but to the fool, good and evil are one and the same."

The Book of Thomas

Techniques

Offering Help

1. Grab yourself a piece of paper and a pen and write down a list of all the people in your life you feel that could benefit from your help.

2. Sit down comfortably, either on a chair or on the floor, with your back straight.

3. Join your hands in prayer position in front of your chest and silently say to yourself, seven times, "May my intuition guide me to who needs my help the most."

4. Without thinking grab your pen and paper and put a star by the the person you intuitively feel could benefit from your help the most.

5. Join your hands in prayer position again in front of your chest and silently say to yourself, seven times, "Over the next three days, may the universe guide me to see, how best to help ... (and say the individual's name) intuitively.

Over the following three days, you should get your answer as a sign, or intuition, or a vision. When you have helped that person you can carry out the exercise again for another individual on the list, helping people one by one.

You Know The Truth

- ❑ Sit down comfortably, either on a chair, or on the floor; make sure your back is straight. Place your palms face down in your lap.

- ❑ Start to breathe in and out very slowly and deeply through your nose, counting for seven on the in breath and for nine on the out breath. Continue with this process for seven minutes.

- ❑ Place the index finger of your right hand in the middle of your forehead, in between your eyebrows, just so it is very lightly touching.

- ❑ Take a deep breath in and press onto your forehead a bit harder. As you breathe out, release the pressure a little. Repeat this five times.

- ❑ Return your right hand to your lap with both your right and left palms facing downwards.

- ❑ Silently say to yourself, with meaning and purpose, eleven times, "May the Universe guide me to know the truth."

- ❑ Place your palms over the top of your chest, at either side and repeat the above statement, seven times.

- ❑ Place your palms over your navel, at either side, so your middle fingers meet at the navel and repeat the above statement, seven times.

- ❑ Place your palms, over your pelvic region, at either side, just below the navel (so your hands are forming a V-shape) and repeat the above statement, seven times.

- ❑ Place your palms over your eyes and repeat the above statement, seven times.

- ❑ Place your palms over your temples and repeat the above statement, seven times.

- ❑ Place your palms, over the base of your skull, at either side, (so you are cupping the back of your head with your palms) and repeat the above statement, seven times.

- ❑ Join your hands in prayer position, in front of your chest and bow with the intention of bowing with humility to the infinite knowledge of your intuition and the Universe.

Seeing Others

 Think of five people that you know. Grab a piece of paper and a pen and write down what sort of people you intuitively feel they are. Complete the exercise below and then see if you still feel you are right about those people. If your perceptions have changed, make a note of this next to your descriptions.

 Lie down comfortably, either on a sofa, the floor or your bed. You can either be on your side or your back for this exercise, whatever feels more comfortable.

 Place your palms over your eyes and take a deep breath in through your nose. As you breathe in visualise a red beam of light coming from up above, as far as the eye can see and entering the top of your head. As you breathe out through your nose see the light come down your neck, along your shoulders and arms, out of your hands and into your eyes. Push the light right into your head. Continue with this process for between fifteen and thirty minutes.

 Maintain your focus and concentration throughout. If your mind wanders, gently bring it back again. Always focus on the red light coming from above you.

 When you have finished, silently say to yourself seven times, with meaning and purpose, "May the Universe guide me to see, the truth inside everyone around me."

Practise this exercise at least three times a week.

It Is Not As Simple As Love Or Fear...

...because emotions are far more complex

A Tall Tale

Honestly, I could write a book about my life experiences. So many odd things have happened to me that I lose track. I was studying to be a chef and feeling really confident about doing it. During one of my classes, I accidentally spilt some boiling water over one of my hands and got some very nasty burns. I was out of action for quite a few weeks so I decided to attend a self-help seminar to sort out some other issues.

The seminar was rather bizarre. The teacher stood up at the front and kept waving his arms around frantically and shouting, "Yeah, are we feeling confident. Say it to me. Tell me you are confident and ready to achieve your potential!" Then he pulled out a ropey CD player, stuck on We Are the Champions, by Queen and insisted that we all sing along.

I tried to hide at the back but he came strolling right up to me, lifted my bad arm into the air and yelled out loud, "Everyone here, you see this man. He has injured his hand." Wow, I thought, someone give him a medal for guesswork. He continued, "There is something that this man wants to do, but he is sabotaging himself with fear. He is afraid of success." Everyone shrieked and whooped at the top of their voices in agreement. I prayed that he would just go away, but I could see he was burning to ask me a question and sure enough, out it popped. "What happened to your hand? What is your dream?" I informed him that I was studying to be a chef and that I had accidentally spilt hot water on my hand. He began nodding furiously and I could just feel another crowd pleaser coming on. He yelled victoriously, "This man wants to be a chef, but secretly he wants to fail. He is trying to sabotage his own success because he is *really* terrified of succeeding. If he would just feel the love and let go of the fear, he could achieve his dreams and you too..." he scanned his eyes across the expectant audience "...could achieve your dreams, if you would just embrace the love and let go of the fear that is preventing your success."

With that, the audience went into hysteria. I was not sure if I was at a rock concert or a cult camp. You could not hear a thing for the slapping of hands, cheering and tears of joy. I could not wait to get out there.

When I left, I had a think about the day's events on the way home. I felt that I had not scalded my hand because I was afraid of success. I had scalded my hand because I was careless. I contemplated the concept of our human emotions and I could not believe that the seminar teacher had tried to constrain the complexities of human emotion into two terms, love and fear. It is just not as simple that. I believe that our emotions are far more complicated.

Seriously Though...

I am going to quote an absolute cult classic. I think I will put this at the number one spot, above the Rolling Stones lyric I utilised in an earlier chapter. You may, or may not, remember a film made in 2001, starring Jake Gyllenhaal and directed by Richard Kelly. The film was called Donnie Darko. I could go into a long-winded discussion about the complex plot, but that would be completely irrelevant. There is an exceptionally cheesy and very sleazy self-help guru in the movie, played by Patrick Swayze, who divides all our emotions into just two poles, love and fear. He gesticulates that everything we do in our lives is a product of one of these two emotions. Donnie, however, is not so easily convinced. In one of his high school classes, he takes a stand against his teacher who is a big fan of Patrick's. She draws a Lifeline diagram on the board, with the two polar extremes representing fear and love.

The teacher distributes cards with specific character dilemmas to all her students and asks each student to place a cross on the line to mark where that dilemma is, in relation to the fear and love options. When it is Donnie's turn he refuses to go through with the exercise stating, "I just don't get this. Everything is lumped into two categories.........Life isn't that simple." When his teacher explains that, "Fear and love are the deepest of human emotions," Donnie responds, "Well, yeah.........ok, but you're not listening to me. There are other things to be taken into account. Like the whole spectrum of human emotion.......People aren't that simple." He later tells her to forcibly insert the Lifeline exercise card into her anus, which is a whole other story, but the movie raises some really good points. There *is* a whole other spectrum of human emotions. Why narrow it down to just two of them?

I just don't know where to start with this one. I think I will begin by stating the absolute obvious. We have a huge range of emotions: love, fear; yes, but also: rational anger and irrational anger, resentment, jealously, greed, desire, hatred, power, unconditional love and conditional love, rational and irrational fears, nervousness, consternation, panic, happiness, joy, bliss, euphoria, friendliness, wonder, unhappiness, guilt, boredom, disdain, shame, confusion, arrogance, wistfulness, contrition, laziness, embarrassment, shock, surprise, wonder, scorn, apathy and the list goes on.

Yes, I am well aware that some of these emotions can be attributed to our fear or our love, but they are not actual fear or love itself. There may be elements of fear or love, but let us not forget the other elements.

Sometimes, people will crave power because they fear the consequences of being powerless, but more often they crave power for many varied and complex reasons. These can include: wealth, control over others, adulation, respect, to instil fear in others, to demonstrate sexual prowess. Some people would say all these are a consequence of underlying fears and in certain cases, they may be. However, there are people who have no fear or love; they just want power for power's sake.

Again, some people are arrogant and this could be a result of their fear and personal insecurities. On the other hand, they may not have any fear or insecurities. They may sincerely believe in their own superiority.

Greed could be a fear of going without or it could just be a physical desire to accumulate wealth, for the reasons mentioned above in regards to power, or for other reasons. Anger could be a fear of facing up to emotional issues or it could be a demonstration of vulnerability, powerlessness or inadequacy, but it could also be due to many other things.

Anger can be rational or irrational. Just because you are angry about something, it does not mean that you are afraid. If you are angry about the state of the world, that anger is rational and it is justified. If you aggressively fly off the handle because someone accidentally broke your biro, it is irrational, but not necessarily based on any fear. It could be purely because you are a big bully. Someone may beat their wife for pure power and desire, without fear or love playing any part whatsoever. Anger can be anger for angers sake, without fear and without love.

The truth is, emotions are multifaceted and intricate. Every situation and circumstance in life is different and what applies to one situation does not necessarily apply to another. It depends on who is involved in the occurrence and what the circumstances are. It also depends on the actions taken.

If I may be so bold as to take it a step further; these 'emotions' have more to do with intuition, or lack of, rather than being products of the mind. Unconditional love is not born out of emotion, but a connection to our souls, to our intuition. Our souls are not products of our minds; they are entities or energies that inhabit our physical bodies until they wither away and die. At this point, our souls take leave from our bodies and embark upon another journey. Our bodies are transitory vessels.

Conditional love is a result of so many factors, like our upbringing, societal conditioning and our environment. Conditional love is not in any way intuitive, but learned from our parents, peers and those around us. If we are only able to love with strings attached, we lack a connection to our souls. Conditional love is a product of the mind or our emotions.

Our souls have no emotions. Whilst our souls inhabit our mortal bodies, if we have a connection to our souls, they converse with our emotions and our physical bodies. The stronger the connection is, the higher the frequency is of our physical and emotional bodies. When the connection is very strong, our physical and emotional bodies implicitly follow the guidance of our souls, presented through the medium of intuition. If we are enlightened we just do as our souls guide us to, without the need of physical or emotional responses to jerk us into action.

When our souls depart from our bodies they exist in a state of heaven (with Divine love), or hell (without Divine love). They know nothing else but this. Unconditional love is not an emotion; it is about having that connection to the soul that allows us to feel that Divine love. If we do not have this soul connection we have only our emotions, or minds and our physical desires to go on. God or the Universe still loves us unconditionally but in the absence of a connection with our souls, we cannot feel that love. This brings up a spectrum of emotions or physical feelings, as we search for the same feeling in other activities in our life. Nothing we do reaches the target because nothing on this earth is in the least bit comparable to the Divine Love we receive from God or the Universe. So, we search and if we do not restore that vital connection, our search is in vain.

Rational fear is very much based on the voices of our souls, our intuition. Our intuition provides a message to kick-start an emotional reaction that manifests as fear, to persuade us to take the appropriate course of action.

Irrational fear comes again from a lack of intuition or from our conditioning and environment. For example, we often fear death because we perceive it as being the end of our existence. If we have a strong intuitive connection to our souls, we understand that the time we spend on this earth is but the blink of an eye compared to the entire journeys of our souls. We know that what we do here plays a huge part in the formation of that journey. Provided we have let right living and right thinking be our tenets for life, we do not fear the aftermath of death, because we know we did the very best that we could. We know that all our souls know is being with or without unconditional love.

Happiness can be attributed to many things, but in reality, true happiness only comes from a connection to our souls, which in turn connects us to God or the Universe. All other bouts of joy and what we term as happiness are fleeting and based on our physical or emotional desires. They only last as long as whatever it is satisfying our desires, at that moment, lasts. For example, I am buying myself a nice new gadget and it makes me happy, but I know full well that a few weeks after I have got it, the novelty will have worn off. It is just a physical object. In real terms it is meaningless.

Unconditional love is *all* that matters to our souls in their purest state when they are without our bodies, but we live in physical bodies in a physical world. Our souls have to communicate with our physical and emotional bodies to get their messages across. If our physical and emotional bodies lack a strong connection with our souls, they are left to fend for themselves, without the necessary wisdom and so, thus, we are affected by so many complex emotions that cannot be ignored or just restricted to love and fear. Yes, love and fear are very deep and profound human emotions, but looking at the bigger picture, there is so much more involved that we cannot even begin to imagine.

At the end of this Chapter, there are some exercises to help you understand your emotions more effectively, by enhancing your intuitive connection. No yawning allowed, I know that a lot of the exercises are geared towards enhancing your connection, but really, nothing in life is more essential that trusting in and following your intuition. The stronger your intuition is, the more balanced your emotions will be and the more rewarding your life will become. Those people, you know the ones, that wander through life cheerily, always appreciating every moment, sharing their joy and gratitude and offering their empathy, we can all be one of those, if we listen to our intuition.

In addition, the exercises are hopefully going to help you get to grips with unconditional love, something we hear about a lot that in reality eludes the many. There is nothing comparable to unconditional love and if you can achieve this state of being, you will have a wonderful sense of happiness and connectedness that no one person can shake.

"Anyone can become angry – that is easy. But to be angry with the right person, to the right degree, at the right time, for the right purpose, and in the right way – this is not easy."

Aristotle

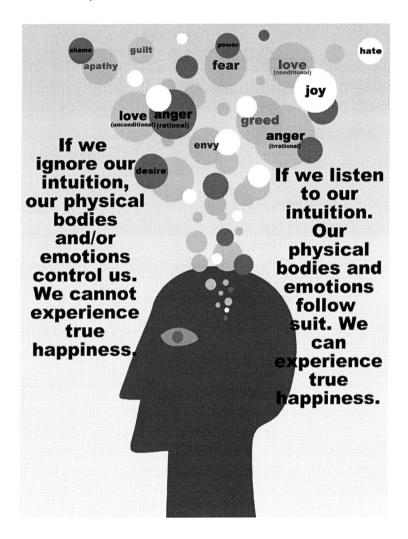

Techniques

Love In Its Purest Form

 When you are lying in bed, before you go to sleep at night, carry out the following exercise.

 Join your hands in prayer position in front of your chest and begin to breathe very slowly and deeply, in and out, through your nose. As you breathe in silently say to yourself, "I breathe in unconditional love." As you breathe out silently say to yourself, "I expel conditional love." Continue this process for between five and fifteen minutes.

 When you have finished, with your hands still in prayer position, silently say to yourself, five times, "Universe please allow me to feel your unconditonal love as I dream. May this feeling stay with me when I awake each day."

Practise this exercise as often as you can.

Pure Intuition

❑ Sit down comfortably, either on a chair, or on the floor; making sure that your back is straight.

❑ Place your left palm over the centre of your forehead, with your fingers pointing upwards towards the ceiling and place your right palm over your navel.

- ❑ As you breathe in slowly through your nose, visualise a bright white beam of light, coming from up above, as far as the eye can see and entering the top of your head.

- ❑ As you breathe out through your nose, push that beam of light down your neck, along your left shoulder, into your left arm, out of your left hand and into your forehead.

- ❑ As you breathe in again, maintain your focus on the light coming from above you and see that light travel down your neck, along your right shoulder, into your right arm and then into the palm of your right hand.

- ❑ Gently holding your breath, visualise the light in your right palm growing bigger and bigger, until it is a ball of white light that is greater than the size of your palm.

- ❑ As you breathe out, push that ball of light into your navel area.

- ❑ Repeat the above five processes, between five and fifteen times.

- ❑ Clap your hands together three times to finish.

Wake Up To Life's Real Purpose...

...because we are here to choose our souls' destinations

A Tall Tale

I never used to believe in anything beyond this life. I thought that this life here was all that we had. I thought that once we died our bodies were buried in the ground and our thoughts and feelings went with it. I lived a pretty reckless life and I barely stopped to think about any of the consequences.

As I got older, my opinions started to change and I read around a bit and came to believe that we were all here to become enlightened. I felt that we were on a journey and one day we would all end up being one mass of energy without any thoughts, feelings or emotions, just existing as energy, in a state of pure bliss. This comforted me and reassured me that I had not made any wrong decisions in life. I ignored the past, hoping that if I denied the past it would simply go away. I carried on pursuing the same old patterns of behaviour, just acting out on those patterns slightly differently.

One day, I was merrily driving along the motorway when before I knew it, I was in a car crash. My car had flipped over. I have to say that I do not remember anything about the accident. All I remember was standing outside the car and seeing myself trapped in there, all covered in blood. There were police cars there and the fire service. Several men were trying to cut me out of the car. I screamed. Why was I seeing myself, what was happening?

I looked around and there seemed to be utter chaos. I banged on car windows on the motorway, as they all sat in traffic, but not one individual could hear me. I felt something behind me and I turned around startled by the sensations. There was nothing there, but I heard a voice saying, "Come with me." It sounded eerie. I suddenly felt as if a wind was rushing past my ear. "Come with me," I heard again, "It will be fun. Remember how much you like having fun."

Before I had time to think, I was surrounded in this terrible darkness, gasping for air. I felt like any love was being torn away from me and my heart felt so cold and empty. Instantly, my life flashed before me. I saw myself making very thoughtless choices and trying to work life for my own personal gain. I was horrified at what I saw. I let out a desperate plea, "I am so sorry for my actions. Please give me another chance." I felt a passing moment of overwhelming love, with no pain or anxiety, just a pure state of perfection.

The next thing I remembered was waking up in the hospital, with my family around me, looking over me and looking jubilant that I had finally come around. They hugged me and I held them back so tightly. It occurred to me in a flash that my choices in life were so important and that I had been given another chance to make the right ones, the ones that would bring me closer to God. I woke up to life's real purpose, realising that we choose the final destinations of our souls', for better or for worse.

Seriously Though...

Why are we here? It is a grand question, one that many of us have struggled throughout the centuries to effectively answer. Some provide better theories than others. I have my own personal theory, but I would not call it a theory, I would call it the truth. You on the other hand, may not, but that is for you to decide. Each of us has all the answers we need for our personal journeys and if we are connected with our souls, we can easily access those answers. If you were to be honest with yourself, you would know why you are here. The truth about our final destinations is Universal. I have heard people say, "This is my truth." That is a cop out to dodge taking any responsibility. There is one truth, the truth of The Universe. We all know it, if we choose to follow our Divine paths.

One theory that has transpired in self-help literature is that we are not here to learn lessons from life, but to recall who we really are. So the theory goes; we know all that we could ever need to know but we are here to experience this for ourselves, because until we actually experience this, it is meaningless.

It is also said by some individuals that God needs to experience God's self in order to find God's self. I would beg to differ. God does not suffer from the kind of human ego that requires any kind of recognition. God is all knowing, all powerful and everywhere at any one moment in time. The need for understanding oneself, is a not a Divine concept. Our souls do know all they need to know for their journeys and we need to have that connection with our souls that we may also know. Before I divulge any further, I am going to discuss some other notions about why we inhabit this planet.

I have heard it said that life is about creating our own reality. We are here to convert our thoughts into this reality and bring our own desires to life. Rather than a series of lessons, life is essentially, in this case, what we make of it. We can either create positive experiences or negative experiences through our thought processes. Again, I am not convinced by this. In fact, human arrogance never fails to exceed my expectations and it does this on a regular basis. I can live with the thoughts have power logic. It makes perfect sense to me that our thoughts are an energy that can have a positive or negative effect on us and our environment. We have certain choices to make in this life and the ability to use our thoughts and intentions as resources helps us to do so. We also have a range of other faculties and as I said in an earlier chapter, our intentions require actions to be of any value.

We cannot however, entirely create our own reality; because as hard we may try to, we are always subject to the will of the Universe. A thought can only become a reality if it is within Divine will. The only way to know if it is within Divine will is to be profoundly intuitive.

Another concept is that we are all here to become enlightened. We live our lives over and over again, in a never-ending circle until we finally embrace enlightenment and then we will no longer require our physical forms because we will exist purely as energy. According to this model we do learn lessons, so that we may eventually become enlightened. If this model was the case though, we would not require any choices in life because we would all be moving towards the same destination anyway. There would be no point in us doing anything or even trying to evolve, if we were all on our way to enlightenment. We cannot *all* be enlightened. We all have the potential to be, but not all of us will, because not all of us want to be.

These are just a couple of ideas, there are so many. In my eyes, the truth of the matter is incredibly simple. Humans are here to become more Divine, or more God like. The way that we do that is to grow spiritually and re-connect to our souls, or strengthen our connections if we already have them. The way for us to achieve this on a physical earth is through learning lessons. We are here to become the Light, to be in the Light, to become one with God or with the Divine. With that, we have a profound choice for our souls' ultimate post-earth destinations; because we do not have to be with the Divine, we can be completely without it. We do not have to be with God's unconditional love when we leave this planet, we can live without it. Whilst we inhabit this earth we make that choice for our souls, through our thoughts, actions and individual choices.

Some of us like to think that we are made in God's image. We do have a Divine spark within and we can choose to completely embrace that Divine spark or reject it. I will leave you to decipher whether you feel we are made in God's image or not, but I will say one thing, we have a darker nature that is far from being Godlike.

To have any kind of a choice, we have to have more than one item to choose from, otherwise we have a given, not a choice. We can choose God or the opposite to God, whatever you deem that to be. Some may prefer to call it the physical or the spiritual. These are the two paths we can walk that I discussed in the chapter on fear. We learn lessons to enable us to make that choice, to take us out of ignorance and into awareness. In ignorance, we do not know that we have a choice, but in awareness we do.

Whether we make the right choice or not, is up to us and what we deem to be the right choice is for each of us to decide, but whatever decision we make here on earth, our souls will live by it.

To add to this, the choice on its own is not enough. We have to live in the right way and think in the right way for that choice to be valid. It is all too easy to say, "Yep I am going to wholeheartedly embrace my spirituality." Anyone can say that without real meaning or deliberation. We have to live by that choice and allow our Divine sparks, our souls to guide us in every single thing that we do. So, good thoughts, right thoughts, are important but they are not enough. They have to become right actions in every aspect of our lives. To know if they are right thoughts and actions we need to totally trust in and follow our intuition and we need to continually learn.

We like to think that the world will last forever and that we have ample time to make our choices, or sometimes we do not even care about those choices, but nothing on this earth lasts forever and that includes the earth itself. In all seriousness, you could write the purpose for us being here on the back of a post card, because it is really that simple. So here it comes.

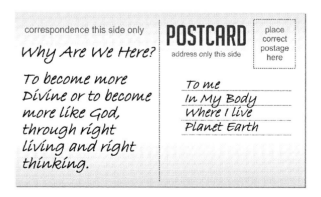

The following exercises will help you to see and know the truth, in time. Finding enlightenment is never easy. I cannot promise you that enlightenment will be yours in an instant. It takes more thought and effort than that. These exercises will get you started though, on finding your right path. The fact that you are attempting the techniques demonstrates that you have a willingness to learn, grow and develop spiritually. That willingness is unquestionably admirable, but it also requires the right thoughts and actions to take place on your part.

If you search hard enough inside of yourself, you will find absolutely all of the answers you need. My words may resonate with you or they may seem like complete rubbish. Ultimately, we all have to make our own choices in life and hopefully these exercises will go towards helping you to make the right ones.

The only thing that helped me to take the right path was Reiki, because it offered an instant connection that I could work from, but still I had to put in hours of dedicated healing and change my life as my intuition guided me to. It was not always easy, but I did it. It will not always be easy for you, but you can do it too, if you really want to.

Jesus said, "Whoever has ears ought to listen. There is light within an enlightened person, and it shines on the whole world. If the light does not shine, it is dark."

The Gospel of Thomas

Techniques

A Real Connection

 Sit down, either on a chair or on the floor; make sure your back is straight.

 Join your hands in prayer position in front of your chest and breathe in and out, slowly and deeply, through your nose, counting for seven on the in breath and counting for nine on the out breath. Continue with this process for a few minutes.

 On your next in breath visualise a thin beam of white light coming from up above, as far as the eye can see and entering the top of your head.

 As you breathe out visualise the light beam in your head travelling down to your heart and then on towards your navel.

 Visualise the beam as a connector and as you breathe in and out, see the light travel from your head, to your heart, to your navel and back again. Intend that a connection is taking place between your spiritual body (head), emotional body (heart) and physical body (navel). Continue with this process for between five and fifteen minutes.

 Bow to the Universe to finish.

Practise this exercise three times a week.

Opening Up

❑   Sit down comfortably, either on a chair, or on the floor; make sure your back is straight. Place your hands in your lap, with your palms facing upwards.

❑   Breathe in through your nose for a slow count of four and out through your mouth for a slow count of four. Continue with this process for three minutes.

❑   As you breathe in, visualise a big red beam of light coming down from up above, as far as the eye can see and entering the top of your head.

❑   As you breathe out, see the light travelling down your neck, along your shoulders and arms and out of your hands.

❑   Continue the above two stages for one minute.

❑   Repeat the above three stages replacing the red light beam with an orange light beam, again for one minute. After this, repeat the process with the following colours, one after the after, each for one minute: yellow, green, blue, indigo, violet, white and gold.

❑   To finish, join your hands in prayer position, in front of your chest, bow forward and then silently say, "May the channels in my body be opened to create a strong spiritual connection that can never be broken."

Life's Purpose

- ❏ Lie down comfortably on your back, either on a sofa, the floor or your bed. Place your palms over your eyes.

- ❏ Breathe in through your nose and as you do so, visualise a beam of gold light coming down from up above, as far as the eye can see and entering the top of your head.

- ❏ As you breathe out very slowly see the gold light travel down your neck, along your shoulders and arms, out of your hands and into your eyes and the back of your head.

- ❏ Continue with the above two processes for between five and ten minutes.

- ❏ Place your palms down by your sides facing upwards and silently say to yourself, with meaning and purpose, fifteen times, "In every moment that I live may the Universe please guide me to see life's purpose."

There Is No New Global Spiritual Consciousness...

...because the state of the world is getting worse

A Tall Tale

I went on a healing workshop last year. The teachers were a bit flaky to be honest and I am not really into all the group hugging and happy clappy singing malarkey. I felt like a bit of an idiot when they pulled me up to the front and suggested that we should rub heart chakras. I had no idea in real terms what that meant, but I was soon to find out that it involved us jumping up and down and banging our chests together voraciously. The whole reason I had attended the workshop was because I was feeling a bit disenchanted with the world and with my life.

The workshop did not change a thing. We sat there at the end of the day's activities, in a circle, holding hands whilst the teachers went into laborious detail about a new spiritual consciousness awakening in the world. They informed us that more new souls were being guided towards a more loving and giving way of life and suggested that at every available opportunity, we should send healing to the whole planet and to all the souls on this earth.

I tried to ask them some very deep and meaningful questions, but they constantly gave me these woolly answers about love and light taking over the planet. I just could not believe what I was hearing. I had totally wasted my money on this stuff. They said that there was no-one who could not be elevated spiritually if they had a little love sent their way. I almost fell about laughing.

On the way home from the workshop, I had a good think about things. I thought about the stories we see on the television news every day and the stories we read in the newspapers. I thought about the people that have crossed my path in life, how especially in modern times there seems to be a distinct lack of courtesy and real compassion for others.

Recent major world events popped into my head, such as: September 9/11, Tsunami, the war on Iraq, the Israel-Lebanon crisis and the dire situation in Afghanistan. I contemplated the state of our government and world leaders. It saddened me to think that people would waste their time and money being convinced that the world was becoming a more enlightened place. At that very moment, I felt a great sense of hope. It occurred to me that whilst the world was far from being a happy, evolved place, I could change my life personally and make a difference on a small scale. I might not be able to single-handedly transform the whole planet but I could make my journey a worthy and more altruistic one. If I could not help everyone, there were people that I could help, in the right way for them.

It is one thing trying to make the world a better place, but it is quite another to live in flagrant blind denial of our own reality. There is no new global spiritual consciousness, as far as I am concerned, because the world is becoming a more unstable place to live in with each new day.

Seriously Though...

For those who believe that humanity as a whole is becoming more evolved and spiritually enlightened and conjecture that the world is becoming a better place, I present ten newspaper headlines from a range of UK newspapers, dated 6th March 2007:

1. Powerful earthquake hits Indonesia – *The Times*
2. $1 million-a-week crack king admits 30 murders – *The Times*
3. Nine civilians 'killed' in US-led air strike – *The Times*
4. Up to 90 dead in Iraq blast – *The Guardian*
5. Briton killed in Afghan Offensive – *The Guardian*
6. Asia Smog 'will melt Arctic ice' – *The Guardian*
7. UK plans to cut CO2 'doomed' – *The Guardian*
8. Up to 30 people 'planned' killing of teenager – *The Telegraph*
9. Iran poised to strike in wealthy Gulf States – *The Telegraph*
10. Young father gunned down for standing up to gangs – *The Daily Mail*

These were just ten particularly unsavoury headlines that the press drummed up, but I had a great many more to choose from. The world is ricocheting out of control. Our belated meagre attempts at damage limitation are falling far short of the dramatic changes that are really needed. We are deluding ourselves, if we believe that a new world consciousness is overtaking the earth.

Without launching into a political debate about the reticence of our governments and big corporations to make any kind of decisive and radical changes, it is obvious to most of us, I think, that the planet is on a steady decline. We often complain about the consequences but we, as human beings, created them. In arrogance many of us have treated the world as our oyster. The danger is that we may swallow it whole. People tend to place such significance on history, but we have consistently failed to learn from it. The same mistakes are being replayed time and time again.

Indubitably, we have become more technologically and economically sophisticated. We are great at accumulating possessions and creating products but in spiritual terms, many people are distinctly lacking. In the Western world we are on a conveyor belt, rushing to work and back every day, locked into a daydream, with our eyes glazed over. In a mad commuter rush we get herded and squashed onto trains and buses. Mechanically, we trundle through each day, working more and more hours than ever before.

We live without thinking about the consequences. We buy our food and many of us do not stop to think where it came from, or how it was generated. We are desperate to achieve our physical desires and will go to enormous lengths to do so.

Our Brave New World soma is drugs (recreational and pharmaceutical) and alcohol. It serves to keep the masses stupefied and in a state of subservience. It prevents them from questioning the way they live their lives. Binge drinking in both the United Kingdom and in the United States is a monumental problem. It often leads to reckless behaviour, a dramatic increase in violence and promiscuous unprotected sex and elevates the number of people with psychological issues.

Our enduring gluttony and drinking habits are costing our national health service billions. According to one study by Professor Barry Popkin, of the Department of Nutrition and Economics at the University of North Carolina, the world's obese population now outnumber the starving. What a terribly sad indictment of the state of humanity.

There are more people with no spiritual connection who will think nothing of sticking a knife in someone for a few pound coins, or even just for the sheer hell of it. We are obsessed with fame, celebrity and models. Many teenagers do not want to be policeman, fireman, doctors or nurses. They want to be catwalk models, reality television contestants and famous hip-hop artists. They want adulation, glory, to rap about guns, drugs and loose women and a shed load of hard cash.

We have become so desensitised to the travesties in the world because we see it so often. We have cast ourselves into self-imposed isolation. Our information is fed to us through a straw called the media and many of us trust it implicitly as being subjective and in our best interests. The horrors and lessons of world disasters are briefly entertained, but even more swiftly forgotten. Many people make token efforts, but the gestures are without meaning and too small to make a real significance.

Our planet is getting hotter every year, the polar ice caps are melting and still we keep chugging out the CO_2 emissions. Nature and the Universe is showing us how easy it can take it all away from us, but we are not really listening, because we will not believe in it until it actually happens. When it does we will beg and pray for forgiveness, for the world to be restored, but will it be too late?

For everything we have in the Western world many of us are feeling like we are struggling to survive, to keep up with the Jones' or just to pay the bills. Some of us think we are being rebellious by indulging in hedonistic pursuits, but in reality, we are in servitude to our own human desires.

We have carefully crafted our very own little Sodom and Gomorrah and most of us are completely oblivious to it as we trundle along in our own little dream world. "It is not so bad," we say. "When has the world ever been perfect?" Never. I am not going to harp on about a bygone era when everything was wonderful. It has become much worse over the years, but it was never perfect, which emphasises my point that we have failed to learn the lessons of history and what makes anyone think that we ever will?

That has cheered you up hasn't it? The doomsayer has called. She is only five foot, two inches and prophesises calamity for us all. It is true that I have painted a very bleak picture but the picture is not a painting, it is our own reality. Now I am going to backtrack a bit. There are people who are making massive endeavours to make this world a better one. They do it with sincerity and love and they truly understand the truth of what I have just said. These people do look beyond the painted picture to the inner reality. They are the real rebels because they hover outside the mainstream quietly trying to make progress in their own significant ways.

More of society is waking up to see the truth. More people are searching for their spirituality and searching for a better way of life. People have had enough of city dwelling and they are escaping in their droves to the countryside to live more simplistic and healthier lifestyles. There are some genuine efforts to protect the planet, to protect each other and make this fragile earth a more liveable place. The organic product industry is booming. Some of this is due to people who really want to make a difference; some is due to big businesses seeing the potential to corner a tidy profit. It has almost become cool to be seen as being 'green.'

However, it may just be too little too late. For all the people who are endeavouring to make a real difference to this world, for all the people who are trying to become better human beings, there are billions more who are not and may never even try.

Hugging a tree, dressing like a hippy and smoking a spliff might be fun, but it is not going to radically change our world, only governments and the populace en masse can achieve that. We as consumers can make conscious choices that force governments and big businesses to bow to our demands, but whether we all will or not, is another matter. Many of us are still being brainwashed and it is hard to break free from our deluded reverie.

By the way, I do not have a problem with people that hug trees or hippies, but there are a whole load of do-gooder new-agers who make out that everything is going to be hunky dory, who resolutely try to convince themselves and others that a wonderful new spiritual consciousness is dawning. In their defence, they would most likely call me a miserable pessimist but am I, or are they in denial? You decide.

Everyone has the potential to grow and evolve, to become more conscious, aware, thoughtful, enlightened and spiritual individuals, whether they would deem themselves to be spiritual or not. Yet, not everyone will, as I have said previously, because not everyone wants to. The next door neighbours who keep playing their music really loud, who verbally abuse the old man at the end of the street, who bully their bull dog to make it aggressive. They do not want to be spiritual, to grow, to make the world a better place. They are slaves to their physical desires. They are cut off from their spiritual nature and their emotions. They live only by their ego.

The gang who shot a seven year kid down the road, do not want to make the world a greener and happier place, they have no compassion. They get kicks out of showing off to their friends and the pain of others affords them immense pleasure.

A despotic world leader does not care a jot about nurturing society and acting for the good of the people. They want their mammoth egos massaged and everything that a physical lifestyle can afford: money, power, praise, cheap thrills, aggression and so the list goes on.

Somewhere, inside some of these sorts of people there may be potential, a slight flicker of compassion and love, but it may never turn into a flame. They may never become enlightened, not because they do not have potential, but because they do not chase after Enlightenment or the most Divine aspects of our human emotions. Instead, they chase after the deepest, darkest side of our human emotions and know nowhere in between.

For others, there is no flicker inside to turn into a flame. Remember the chapter on trying to see the good in people, or not as the case may be. Some people will never be good, so there is no use trying to draw any good out of them. You cannot find what is not, and was never, there.

This is not to say that we should completely give up trying. Worthy causes are always worth fighting for, if we do it with genuine love and sincerity. We are here to nurture our souls and steer them towards the Divine. Our thoughts and actions are fundamental to the paths of our souls. We are all unconsciously choosing our destinations with every single step we take in life. If we can make footprints in the sand and at least try to make a difference, that is fantastic. The key is to make a difference where we can, to help the people that we can genuinely help, rather than wasting our time on those we cannot.

The most important thing we can do on this earth is to follow the guidance of our souls, to (here it comes again) trust in our intuition. It sounds so damn obvious, but for so many of us it is not an easy task. We cannot quieten the other voices that occupy our busy minds and we cannot decipher our rational reasoning from our emotions or our emotions from our intuition. We fool ourselves into believing that we are working based on intuition, when we are not even sure what our intuition sounds like. We blame human actions on animal instincts, screaming, "They are behaving like animals."

You have probably guessed by now that I do not subscribe to evolution theory. It is, after all, a theory and we have many of those. I cannot see that it would be possible for fish to one day crawl out of the sea and if they did, why are they not doing it right now? Why are monkeys not still evolving and why are we not evolving?

Big Bang theory is just another theory. Much of science is based on human hypothesis and no human being alive today was there at the beginning of the formation of our planet to provide any unquestionable scientific validity to these sorts of theories.

There are some scientists who believe and who have believed in God, or a supreme force, in one form or another. These have included: Nicholas Copernicus, Robert Boyle, Sir Francis Bacon, Johannes Kepler, Max Planck, Galileo Galilei, Rene Descartes, Isaac Newton, Gregor Mendel and Albert

Einstein. Although Einstein could not conceive of a personal God, he could neither conceive of a Universe that had not been created.

Isaac Newton believed that the beauty, intricacy and order of the Universe could, "Only proceed from the counsel and dominion of an intelligent and powerful being." He also stated that, "The Supreme God exists necessarily, and by the same necessity, he exists always and everywhere." [3]

I cannot believe that anyone can look up at the stars, at the beauty and elegance of the Universe and not consider that they may be a greater force at work, a force that is too great for us to comprehend.

In our human arrogance, we see ourselves as being at the top of the chain, but the choices we make put us right at the bottom. Animals and humans differ in a fundamental way and that phenomenal difference is that we have the ability to make choices. Animals act on their instincts for survival. We squander ours.

We have wisdom, knowledge, awareness and choices. We can choose not to act on our anger, not to rely purely on our base physical desires. We can choose to steer ourselves towards real spiritual evolution, but instead, many of us choose to wallow in the mud, when the heavens are shining down on us to show us a way out of the quagmire. If we are not careful the mud will turn into quick sand and we will not have the choice of escaping.

I am not a saint, some people from my past would no doubt testify to that. I have lived my life very thoughtlessly, recklessly and irresponsibly in the past, but I realised the error of my ways. I found the real meaning of happiness and

---

[3] *Principia*, Book III; *Newton's Philosophy of Nature: Selections from his writings*, p 42, ed. H.S. Thayer, Hafner Library of Classics, NY, 1953.

I clawed back a connection with my intuition. It was not easy but I did it and there is no reason why you cannot do it too.

We are not expected to be perfect, just to take steps in the right direction. We need to see what is genuinely there, rather than what our eyes want to see. We need to hear what is there, rather than what our ears want to hear and we need to do what we should do, rather than just what we want to do.

The world is exquisitely beautiful and you only need to hear a bird sing or watch a flower bloom to know that, but stick your head out of the car window and listen hard to the police sirens roaring and breathe in the smoggy air. We had something so perfect, but we have broken it and day by day, we destroy it even more. The world is not ours to destroy and if we ravage it, it will in turn ravage us.

So, I say kick the utopian wishful thinking, wake up and smell the truth. We are turning our once beautiful world into a dystopian nightmare. We might not be able to save it completely but we do have choices to make, we can make an effort. Even if we cannot save the world in the end, some of us can rescue our poor beleaguered souls and surely that is worth the effort.

I know it all sounds so bleak but the truth often is. We can sit down depressed and do absolutely nothing about it, wallowing in our own self-pity or we can get up and make our lives better, helping others in the process. Yeah the truth is harsh, but it is also wonderful in so many ways. Blind resignation is causing so many catastrophes in the world but if we take some positive action, we can shed some light for others, give more people greater choices and cultivate our personal growth for the benefit of our souls and for the good of humanity.

The exercises at the end of this chapter, if practised regularly, will help you to have faith in you, to have faith in your own wisdom. This could one day enable you to perceive the absolute truth of the Universe in all its profound glory and grace and in all its disgrace and deformity.

The earth did not have to be an ugly place but we made it that way. We owe it to the earth, to the Universe and to our souls to be utterly honest with ourselves, to accept the reality of the world in which we live and to at least *attempt* to change that reality for the good of all humankind. There is no new global spiritual, consciousness awakening. The world is becoming a challenging and dangerous place to inhabit, but some of us can rise above that to a greater spiritual awareness and those of us who can, should do it today, whilst we still have the chance.

"It has become appallingly obvious that our technology has exceeded our humanity."

Albert Einstein

Techniques

Inner Wisdom

 Sit down comfortably, either on a chair or on the floor; make sure your back is straight. Join your hands in prayer position in front of your chest.

 Concentrate on the feeling of your palms pressed together and breathe in and out very slowly and deeply through your nose. Continue focusing on your palms for three minutes.

 Silently say to yourself, with meaning and purpose seven times, "I accept the reality, the truth that lies before me. May my inner wisdom always guide me."

 With your hands still in prayer position, focus on the middle of your forehead, between your eyebrows (third eye) for three minutes.

 Still focusing on that area, silently say to yourself, with meaning and purpose, seven times, "I am realising my Divine purpose on earth."

 Place your palms over your eyes and repeat the above statement seven times.

 Bow to the Universe to finish.

Practise this exercise five times a week.

My True Path

- ❑ Carry out this exercise when you are resting in bed, before you go to sleep. Keep a notebook and pen by your bed as you will need it when you wake up. Place your left palm over your navel and your right palm on top of your left palm.

- ❑ Breathe in through your nose very slowly and deeply for a count of nine and out through your mouth very slowly for a count of nine. Continue with this process for five minutes.

- ❑ Keep your left palm where it is and place your right palm at the bottom of your chest, in the centre.

- ❑ Silently say to yourself, with meaning and purpose, eleven times, "May the Universe please guide me to see my true path in life, in my dreams."

- ❑ Place your palms over your eyes and repeat the above statement.

- ❑ Place your left palm back over your navel, with your right palm on top and visualise the whole room engulfed in a bright gold light. Allow that light to permeate your entire body. Focus on this image for three to five minutes, before drifting off to sleep.

- ❑ When you wake up grab your notebook and pen and write down any dreams that you can remember vividly, or vivid aspects of the dreams if you cannot recall everything.

❑ After this, silently say to yourself, with meaning and purpose, eleven times, "May the Universe guide me towards the meaning of these dreams, if I need to understand may the answers come to me."

Do not dwell on the dreams you have had, or mull over them. The answers will come to you as and when you need them, so once you have had the dreams and made a note of them, let them go. You may find as you go back to re-read them and write down new dreams that some of the meanings become apparent at that point.

Remember to take note of the intuitive guidance you are given and do not always take dreams for face value.

Practise this exercise on two nights a week, for two months. Have a break for three months and then practise again on two nights a week for two months and so on.

Of Great Significance

❑ Grab some paper and a pen for this technique. Write down headings from some major world events that you can think such as: September 9/11, Tsunami, Hurricane Katrina, the war on Iraq, the earthquakes in Indonesia and some more recent occurrences, depending on what year you are reading this book in!

❑ Under each event on your list, write down some reasons why you think this event happened, not just on a human level but on a Universal level. What could these events symbolise? How has the world changed since these events? What do these events mean for humanity? Write down whatever comes to you and whatever feels intuitive to you.

❑ Carry out the exercise below and then come back to your list and see if you can add anything else or change it. Keep a hold of your list and as new insights come to you and new major world events occur, add them to your list. See how your thoughts on what these events mean change, over time. Try to always consciously be aware of what is going on around you and what significance it holds. Try to look far beyond the surface to a deeper and more Universal symbolism.

Universal Knowledge

❑ Sit down comfortably, either in a chair, or on the floor; make sure your back is straight.

❑ Place your left palm over the middle of your forehead, with your fingers pointing upwards and place your right palm over the top of your chest, at the centre.

❑ Breathe in through your nose and as you do so, visualise a white beam of light coming down from up above and entering the top of your head.

❑ As you breathe out through your nose, push the light down your neck, along your shoulders and arms, out of your hands and into your head and chest areas. Repeat the above two steps for five to fifteen minutes.

The World Is Very Real...

...because the world really does exist

A Tall Tale

I was ill for many years. I had no idea what was causing the illness and I did very little about it. The doctors could not find anything wrong with me and for a long time I just gave up on getting better. This all changed when I read a book about our diseases and pain being an illusion, a product of our thoughts. I became convinced that my illness did not really exist. I thought that if I ignored it and maintained to myself that I was healthy, it would go away.

My friends and family thought I was crazy, because for so long I had been talking about my illness and suddenly

I was not mentioning it at all. If anyone brought it up in conversation, I would very quickly change the subject.

After a year of doing this and feeling slightly better, I started to feel very unwell again, only this time it was much worse. I noticed a hard lump developing in my stomach area and eating and holding down food was becoming incredibly difficult. My family became terribly worried and insisted that I go to see a doctor. Eventually I caved in to their demands.

I had a biopsy and the oncologist informed me that I had stomach cancer. I was in a state of complete shock. After chemotherapy treatments failed, he told me that I only had a few months left to live. I was horrified and so mad at myself for trying to convince myself that my illness was not real. If I had taken action earlier I could have been cured.

I am on my last legs now. I cannot get out of bed and I cannot hold any food or even liquids down. All of my hair has fallen out from the chemotherapy treatments I had. I am permanently attached to a drip. I am ready to die and I am sure that it will happen in a few days.

I have finally made peace with myself, but I realise that I was foolish to try and ignore my own ill health. I am in chronic, excruciating pain. Is my pain an illusion? Absolutely not. Perhaps when I die this pain will go away, but for now it is all too real and I would advise anyone to take action if they have problems or issues, rather than pretending that they do not exist.

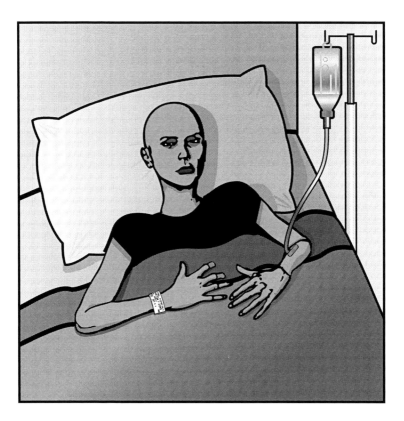

Seriously Though...

Some self-help experts and renowned spiritual teachers hold the belief that our personal problems, illnesses, injuries and even the planet are some kind of illusory state of being. Yes, that's right, if you fall over and break your ankle it is not *really* broken you are merely imagining it and by feeding the notion that your ankle bone *is* broken, you prevent yourself from healing. I think this idea is crazy, but that's just me.

So the idea goes, illnesses, problems and injuries are not real and thus, no solution is required. If you try to solve any of these issues by trying to make them vanish you are incorrectly assuming that there is something that needs fixing in the first place.

Where you are apparently going so very wrong is that it doesn't need fixing, because everything is perfect as it is and if we accept this as the truth, our minds are freed from the burden of fear, which is replaced by unconditional love. In turn our physical experiences alter according to this new state of mind. The 'logic' behind this all boils down to the Law of Attraction, as far as I can see, the idea that we control our physical, material world through our thoughts. Thus, if you tell yourself your illness is already cured, it will be so. If you combine this with the Law of Least Effort or in Taoist terms, Wu Wei ('effortless doing') you can sit around on your backside all day pretending that nothing is real and doing and achieving absolutely nothing. See how far it gets you.

Back to our illusory problems, my thoughts on this concept are that the world is very real and your experiences, problems, illnesses and injuries are entirely real. If you have cancer, you have a life draining tumour inside your body and ignoring its presence will not cure it. I feel that if we assume that our problems are just figments of our imagination we are in grave danger of not taking responsibility for our actions.

Our problems and illnesses do require solutions and the best way to solve them is through using our thoughts and turning those thoughts into restorative actions that bring us back to health and well-being. Our illnesses, problems and injuries exist for a variety of reasons, including: our lifestyles, our environment, our relationships with other people, our dietary habits, our emotional traumas and our stress levels. To effectively deal with our problems we need to address the causes and take active steps in the right direction. Pretending that our illnesses do not exist will not make them disappear.

Someone who has lung cancer and smokes sixty cigarettes a day, may well intend that the disease is not there, or that it is cured, but unless they kick the nicotine habit, their thoughts will not manifest into reality.

If you pretend that illnesses are imaginary, there are no guarantees that you will never develop an illness. In fact, you probably will get ill at some point in your life. The world is tainted, polluted and chock-full of manmade toxic substances. With the best will in the world, it is incredibly unlikely that we can avoid illness for our entire lives. The world is sickly through both human action and inaction and by damaging the earth, we damage ourselves.

There *is* often a marked difference between what we perceive to be real and what is real in the greater scheme of things. For instance, what people view as the key to ultimate happiness and contentment, is often quite different from the true route to fulfilment. Yet, this does not make anyone's experiences invalid or incorrect. They are real at that moment in time, based on where that person is physically, emotionally and spirituality. It is not the world or pain or suffering that is the illusion, but people's perception of those things.

If you have an illness it is real. How you deal with that illness is based on your perception of it. You might give up and just let it take you over, or change your lifestyle to a healthier one and work towards health. Your perception of that reality will affect the final outcome, but it won't make your experiences any less real.

On the issue of perception and how we all perceive the world, the more spiritually aware we become, the more our perception resembles the truth. When we achieve a state of enlightenment our perception *is* the truth. Until we come to rely on our intuition, our perception is inherently flawed, because we view everything through our other physical and emotional faculties, which possess neither the insight of our intuition, or the Divine knowledge. We lack the ability to see the bigger picture. Once we have reached a certain point on our spiritual paths, we develop a much higher awareness and understanding of the Universe.

So, in short, it is not the world or our pain, suffering or experiences that are an illusion, but we may have an inaccurate perception of those things, if we are not guided by our intuition. Whether you feel your illness will be the end of you, or whether you feel that it is an opportunity for personal growth, you are still unwell. Your physical body is damaged and that *is* real. It needs to be dealt with immediately. Your personal perception of what your condition means for you physically, emotionally and spiritually, may not be correct. It can only be truly accurate, if it is based on intuition.

Talking of reality and illusion, there is one big illusion that some people hold dear and that illusion is that the world is perfect. We just make it imperfect through our thoughts, because our thoughts construct our reality.

Everything is **not** perfect. In fact it is far from perfect. We would not be here right now if the world were flawless. Human beings are inherently flawed by their own corporeality. Human perfection resides in the inner Divine sparks within, our souls. Aside from that, we are far from being perfect. In perfection we would have nothing to learn, but we have everything to learn and it is essential for us to acknowledge this for our own spiritual evolution.

An individual may decide to sit back and accept their own perfection and by this token feel that they need to take no positive steps in life because they are already where they need to be. Perfection or as I would call it, enlightenment, requires right thinking and right living. It requires aspiring and working towards unconditional love. We are not perfect already. You are not perfect already. I am not perfect already. We have much work to do. We have to learn and we have to aspire towards perfection in everything we do in our lives, in every thought, step and action we take. Perfection is not a given that we just have to accept. It is earned.

In true humility I feel that we should accept that we are not aware enough as souls to even comprehend the true significance of what it means to be perfect. We can of course speculate and dare to assume. We can grow closer to a more enlightened state and some of us can achieve enlightenment. However, the completeness of enlightenment is *still* not the truest perfection that exists. To me that immaculate title is reserved for God. Even if you do not believe in God, I am sure you can recognise your own fallibility and understand that even stripped of your flesh shell, you are not completely perfect...yet.

Another notion that seems way off the mark is the idea that the physical body is just an imaginary projection of the mind or more precisely, the ego. Poor old ego, I defend its presence in a later chapter. So, your body is not real at all. No wonder your illnesses are non-existent. The body is real, somebody pinch me here. I think we need to free ourselves from the idea that we are completely masters of own reality. As I have said many times before, we are subject to the will of the Universe and we have far less control than we could ever possibly imagine. When we follow our higher paths, we become freer and happier and then we relinquish rather than coveting control. Ask a friend to give you a shove and it will feel incredibly real.

Our bodies are temporal and our souls are infinite, so the life we lead here is fleeting, but our journeys here are precious and dictate where our souls will reside after we leave this planet. This does not make our bodies insignificant, or an illusion.

To take this concept further, if you believe in God and you believe that God created the earth, why would you suppose that he would create something illusory? The idea that this world of ours is an illusion devalues our journeys on earth and devalues what our souls are here to achieve on this physical earth.

It has been claimed that our souls know no pain. It is only our physical bodies that experience pain, which is odd because the same theory speculates that our problems are not real, so surely we are not really experiencing pain. Well, so the argument goes, our physical pain is imagined. The pain, suffering, violence, destruction and degradation of the planet are viewed as sheer imagination, a product of our thoughts.

Some people who have adopted this point of view avoid reading newspapers, watching television, listening to the radio and so on, to prevent perceiving these things as a reality. I beg the question, if these events are not realities, what is the issue with reading or hearing about them? If they are an illusion, reading or hearing about them shouldn't make any difference, because they are not real anyway.

The world is real, the catastrophes, disasters and lack of compassion in the world are real. Human beings created all these things and it is up to human beings to correct them. Again, we need to take responsibility for ourselves. We may, as a species, create these realities through warped perception and actions, but they are real none-the-less. The world would still exist if there were no human beings inhabiting it. This planet existed before humankind ever set foot upon it. The world does not exist by virtue of our thoughts. If we all lost the ability to think, the world would still be real and it would still exist, *we* just would not know about it.

This life we have here is intrinsic to the journeys of our souls and our souls are not free from pain and suffering. They are painfully burdened with the suffering of our human existence. Every single time we make a decision that takes us away from our intuition we diminish the ties with our souls and our souls suffer intensely because of this. Our physical, emotional and spiritual bodies are deeply interconnected and we cannot affect one without affecting the other two.

If we damage ourselves physically or emotionally, our spiritual bodies are blighted as well. If we consistently flout the intuitive guidance of our souls, we can cause irreparable damage to our energy bodies. So, I would like to suggest that the world is real, we are real and our pain is real, to both our physical bodies and our souls.

The exercises at the end of this chapter will help you to understand your own reality and by elevating yourself and Universal awareness, the techniques will enable you to readily distinguish between truth and fiction. There will come a time, if you practise the exercises enough, when you feel that you have all the answers you need for your journey on earth. You will strongly perceive the voice of your intuition, instead of clutter and confusion reigning over your mind.

"Reality isn't the way you wish things to be, nor the way they appear to be, but the way they actually are."

Robert J Ringer

Techniques

Truth Perception

 Sit down comfortably, either on a chair, or on the floor; make sure your back is straight. Place your palms in your lap, facing upwards.

 Breathe in slowly your nose and out slowly through your mouth, counting to five on each in breath and counting to nine on each out breath. Continue this process for three minutes.

 Join your hands in prayer position, in front of your chest, with your thumbs pressed against your sternum.

 Silently say to yourself, with meaning and purpose, seventeen times, "May I see the truth of my life and the world."

 Place your palms over your eyes and repeat the affirmation above, seventeen times.

 Place your left hand over the base of your skull and your right hand over your forehead and repeat the affirmation, above seventeen times.

 Bow to the Universe to finish.

Practise this exercise five times a week.

The Real World

- ❑ Grab some paper and a pen for this technique. Write down a list of ten of your of beliefs on the real or illusory nature of the world and our experiences. Write down why you feel these things are real or illusory.

- ❑ Sit down comfortably, either on a chair, or on the floor; make sure your back is straight. Place your hands in prayer position, in front of your chest.

- ❑ Read out the first item on your list and your reason for having that particular belief.

- ❑ Close your eyes and breathe in and out, very slowly and deeply, through your nose, counting to five on the in breath and five on the out breath. Continue with this process for five minutes, retaining the belief in your head for the entire time.

- ❑ Silently say to yourself, with meaning and purpose, eleven times, "May the Universe guide me to see the reality behind this personal belief."

- ❑ Repeat the above three steps, for each belief on your list, reading it out, following the breathing exercise and then reciting the affirmation.

- ❑ Bow to the Universe to finish.

Practise this exercise at least once a week. You will find that over time your beliefs may start to change, in line with your more profound intuitive connection.

Spirituality Is Not Just About What You Say...

...because spirituality is about what you actually do

A Tall Tale

I was never particularly interested in anything esoteric, but one Saturday, my friend persuaded me to go and visit a tarot card reader. I was slightly hesitant and sceptical initially, but eventually she managed to twist my arm. I had no idea what to expect. I just tagged along to keep my friend company.

When we arrived at the tarot card reader's house, I began to feel a bit nervous about what she was planning on telling me.

My friend had a reading first. Afterwards, she came rushing out saying, "Oh it was so amazing. You will enjoy it." This calmed me down considerably and I actually felt a pang of excitement.

I sat down in front of the lady reading the cards and she laid out a spread of cards on the table in front of me. I had no clue what significance any of them actually had. She started asking me loads of questions about my life, which seemed suspicious, considering that she was supposed to be psychic. "Are you in the advertising field?" I did give her an affirmative response, but then I had told her beforehand that I was in a very creative industry and that I had to come up with ideas. "Are you thinking of going travelling this autumn, somewhere where the temperature is quite hot, but not too overbearing?" Well give the lady a prize. I was but it seemed so generalised. "You have a son don't you?" I offered a negative response, but not to be put off she continued, "Well then, one of your best friends has a son and he is about to start at secondary school." She was indeed correct but I failed to see the relevance of her very mundane offerings. Surely, the spirit world had something more profound to convey to me, than where I was going on holiday and what industry I worked in.

The icing on the cake was when she said, "You are going to find love in the most unexpected of circumstances, sometime next June." Blimey, what a lucid and useful précis of my life. I could not understand what my friend had been so terribly excited about, but apparently she had asked the tarot card reader if she was going to get her dream job this year and she gave a positive response.

I felt like I had been completely ripped off to be perfectly honest. I am not saying that all psychics or tarot card readers are frauds, but I do believe that some of them have questionable motives and lack any real kind of intuition. I believe that spirituality has so much more to do with living your life in the right way and trusting your intuition. The other stuff is really not so important and I will think twice next time before I give my hard earned cash to a so called 'expert' in the spiritual realm. I am going to stick to trusting myself instead and give the crystal balls and magic cards a wide berth.

Seriously Though...

We have a self-help century. Increasing numbers of people are desperate for ways to alleviate their stress, enhance their well-being and find accurate spiritual guidance. There are so many self-help and spiritual books out today that the market is becoming saturated. It is brilliant that so many people are looking for ways to improve their health and well-being. It is fantastic that people want to change their lives for the better.

On the other hand, spirituality, like being seen to be 'green,' does seem to have turned into a consumer exploit, a fashion trend, a badge you can parade around in and boast about your spiritual credentials to others. I practise Reiki and there are plenty of Reiki teachers who perceive their title as a badge of honour and they like to show off to their pals or peers with pointless tricks, like trying to improve the taste of wine by healing it and fixing their broken household objects with Reiki. As human beings, we like gimmicks it would seem and they often appeal above and beyond taking real actions to change our lives for the better.

There are a great many books about spirituality out there. Some of the information is exceedingly helpful, some is marginally useful and some is exploitative and gimmicky. Of course readers need to be given some credit to sort the wheat from the chaff, but there are many people who really *do* believe something just because they read it in a book.

The key is, to be discerning. Trust in whatever feels right to you and forget about the rest. Spirituality is not about qualifications, calling yourself a spiritual guru, or claiming to have a wealth of practical experience in the spiritual arena. Just because someone has written thirty books, or claims that they are a spiritual or guru it does not necessarily indicate that they possess wisdom or insight to any degree. There may be some truths, there may be half truths, or there may be no truths whatsoever in the words that they proffer. Spirituality is about the way we live our lives. Without spiritual actions to back up all our proclamations we just have airy fairy, empty concepts that lack any real significance.

We are frequently told that everyone is intrinsically spiritual and whilst there is a sliver of truth in this, because human beings possess a Divine spark within, many people do not capture this spirituality. Potential alone is not enough.

Wisdom is not born out of our life experiences *per se*. It comes from following our intuition. As we grow older we like to think that we are wiser, but we only become wiser if we have *learned* from our mistakes in life through *following* our intuition. You can have had a wealth of life experiences and never learned a damn thing from any of them, making you very unwise indeed. You can glean more intuitive insight from some five year olds than fifty five year olds, because children can often have a stronger spiritual connection. Life has not worn them down yet.

We should not judge peoples' spiritual credentials on what they *say* they are or what they *say* they have done. We should not judge our own spirituality by the same measure. Spirituality is about how you *live* your life. It is most definitely not about how you tell other people you live your life.

What astonishes me is that some individuals seem to think that having a penchant for the psychic realm of ghosts, spirits, angels, and past lives, or adorning crystals and floaty smocks can be passed off as being spiritual. Not a chance, being a spiritual person is a lifestyle choice. There are people who have made that choice without ever uttering the word spirituality. They live their lives according to their intuition, making good choices that foster their spiritual growth. The flaky, airy fairy stuff, such as wearing crystals, looking into a crystal ball or delving into past lives is pseudo-spirituality. It is not what spirituality is really about. It is also a sure fire way to alienate the majority of people who prefer a more practical approach.

I have a bone to pick with spiritual teachers, healers and other such individuals who claim to be immeasurably wise and then, indulge in hedonistic activities which would suggest otherwise. Those who claim to be spiritual teachers or healers need to practise what they preach. For instance, if you tell me that you are a lap dancer and a spiritual leader, healer or guru, I will fail to be convinced. If you allege that you are a spiritual teacher and then spend your evenings chasing the dragon, I am not going to be duped. You do not see the Dalai Lama moonlighting as an escort.

I have done some exceptionally *unspiritual* things in my lifetime, but at the time I was doing them, I would never have called myself spiritual, because it would have been a barefaced lie.

To be genuinely spiritual, you have to live the life that goes with it. There are no ifs and buts. If you say you are spiritually enlightened, but you do not live the life, then your claims are very dubious. An enlightened soul is in a state of awareness and consciousness. If you are enlightened, you will have no desire to do anything that could potentially damage your spiritual path, nor will you be able to, because your intuition will reign so supreme over you that it will just not permit that sort of behaviour.

Excessive drinking, taking drugs, having promiscuous sex, getting your kit off for the lads or indeed the ladies and parading legs akimbo around a stage, levitating an ashtray to impress your friends, going to the pub every night or any night, eating meat like it is going out of fashion, are not the activities of the enlightened. If anyone wants to do any of those things, fine, be my guest, but they should not then proclaim to be enlightened and spiritual souls. Beyond that they should not be misleading others.

So for the 'spiritual gurus' who talk the talk but do not walk the walk, I have to say, put down your pint of beer, line of Charlie and your box of iced doughnuts, get off of your high horse and get back into the play pen with all the other unenlightened souls. Meow, a saucer of milk for me I think.

Now I am going to get down off of my high horse, hopefully without getting my feet caught in the stirrups. The somewhat severe assertions above apply to exploitative and disingenuous, spiritual teachers or healers, who claim to have amassed a wealth of spiritual knowledge and wisdom, but fail miserably to live by it. For all the other people, you are not expected to give up eating meat or to stop socialising with your friends, or stop doing the things that you enjoy in life. What you should be doing is fostering your spiritual path so that the things you enjoy are the things that are right for you, at that moment in time.

You do not have to stop doing everything at once. It is a gradual process as you develop. As you become more aware and as you enhance your intuitive connection changes will take place very naturally. It will not be something that has to be forced or that will feel challenging. The changes will just happen at the right time for you and as they do so, everything will fall into place. When you develop, you do not want to do those very physical desire driven things anyway because they do not contribute to your spiritual growth. They take you away from it.

For my own personal path I felt guided to become vegan, quit drinking alcohol, eat predominantly organic foods and stop going to pubs and clubs. That was my path and my personal guidance. You do not necessarily need to do those things. Your path is just that, your path, and you need to do what your intuition prescribes. If giving up something feels like a real chore or sacrifice, you may need to work on your spiritual growth a bit more until the necessary changes feel more effortless. Just be sure that you are doing what your intuition prescribes, rather than pursuing purely physical or emotional desires.

For those who already are or who want to be spiritual teachers, your level of teaching ability will depend on how far you have progressed on your spiritual journey. Your level of wisdom will reflect how far you are along this spiritual path. Your wisdom may be nada if you have made no progression at all. Your wisdom may be partially useful to a degree if you have made good progress, or your wisdom may be superb if you have devoted yourself wholeheartedly to your spiritual path. Ultimately though, as individuals, we need to trust in our own intuition above and beyond what anyone ever tells us. The insights of others can be helpful but they are not always cast in stone and however insightful they may be, your intuition is always your greatest guide.

We also need to remember that our insights, whilst relevant to our own personal spiritual paths, may not always be applicable on a Universal scale. We have to very carefully distinguish between the knowledge that is intended for us and the knowledge that is to be shared with everyone. There is some wisdom that we will never be able to convey to others, as long as we inhabit this earth. This wisdom is purely for us to know. We also need to understand how to share what we know with others, according to their own personal spiritual paths.

The quest for our true spiritual natures can be a magnificent journey, if we just go about it in the right way and understand that saying we are going to do something, or saying we are spiritual is not enough. Spirituality is so much more than that. We are spiritual if we let right thinking and right living become our life principles, regardless of whether we or any other individual says we are spiritual or otherwise.

Spiritual Consumerism

You will probably have noticed that I have taken issue with a lot of things and my next bone of contention is with what spirituality has come to represent in the twenty-first century. There are an increasing number of people drawn to what we deem to be spiritual pursuits but I feel that we use the term spirituality too liberally.

The online Cambridge Dictionary defines the word spirituality as, "The quality of being concerned with deep, often religious, feelings and beliefs, rather with the physical parts of life." In stark contrast, what I think we are witnessing is an ever growing spiritual consumerism. People seem to want the peripheral aspects of spirituality without the conscience and the core. Many people don't seem to want to take responsibility for their lives or make profound changes in their patterns of thinking and behaviour. They want to know if they were Marie Antoinette in a past life, or if the tarot cards are forecasting wealth and material abundance. Perhaps they like wearing a crystal around their neck because it gives them special powers, or 'heals' them with no effort involved. It makes them seem a bit kooky and spooky and different to everyone else.

If someone wishes to adorn their body with crystals, I have no problem with that, as long as they understand that the crystal is just an object for decoration. It is not actually doing anything, apart from sitting there, looking pretty.

Seriously though, how many people can have been Marie Antoinette, Joan of Arc, King Henry VIII, William the Conqueror, in their past lives? Was no one ever a peasant, sailor, soldier or a prostitute? Is every individual who feels called to change the world for the better, feels compelled to heal others, feels that spiritual techniques can heal anything, has had harsh life experiences and feels that are here for a higher purpose, really a Lightworker or angel? People like to have a sense of their own self-importance. Being told that we were once a magnificent person or that we are a Lightworker can make us feel worthwhile and special. It gives us a sense of purpose in life.

The reality is that we are all special and magnificent, regardless of what we were in a past life or in this life. We all have a valid purpose for inhabiting the earth and the true magnificence lies in us fulfilling that purpose, whatever it may be.

We should feel valuable and precious because we are, not because of what we have been told. Everyone has a different path in life and everyone has their own purpose and whatever it is, they should embrace their purpose and live by their intuition, with a great sense of humility in the face of God or the Universe. Maybe you are a Lightworker or angel, maybe you are not. Maybe you were once Joan of Arc in a past life, maybe you were not. Follow your path. That is what matters in this life. If you do this, you will come to truly understand who you are and you will value yourself because of that realisation.

Shops are popping up all the over the place with the tools to be a 'spiritual' person. Individuals often claim to be spiritual without any thoughts of the necessary implications of this, without a thought for the actions and choices they have made in life. Humanity is very much desire driven, yet simultaneously it stretches out an eager arm to dip into the spiritual realm and it extracts whatever it fancies.

Celebrities initiate the trends and many of them have happily hopped onto the spirituality shopper bandwagon. I happened to be flicking through the television channels a while back, when I came across a bizarre programme about celebrities and religion. It did not surprise me in the least to see that certain celebrities rush to purchase bottles of healing water, allegedly infused with healing Rabbi meditations. This supposedly imbues the H2O with miraculous powers. Wow, if that is the case, please send a truck load to some disaster survivors, not only will their thirst be quenched but their ailments healed. We had better start stocking the stuff in our supermarkets. The world could do with some healing.

What on earth happened to 'right' living and simply offering unconditional love? I am not a religious person, as such, but I believe that the words in the Bible, "Our love must not be a thing of words and fine talk. It must be a thing of action and sincerity" [4] to be profoundly true.

Wearing a bracelet, drinking energy drinks infused with prayer and parading around in a blinged out crucifix are not going to save the world, unless I am missing something

---

[4] John 3:18 (New Revised Standard Edition.)

here. They are not expressions of true spirituality. As far as I can see, many of these sorts of things are just gimmicks, produced to make a nice tidy little profit.

A number of famous hip-hop stars adorn themselves with million dollar jewel encrusted crosses, as if the size of their jewellery is an accurate reflection of their spirituality and commitment to God. They stand in a circle with the back stage crew and band, before they head on stage and pray that they will give a great performance. All the while, they are rapping about popping caps in peoples' rear ends, having sex with libertine women and dropping pills.

What is even more astonishing is that some people seem to worship celebrities as if they were heavenly, Divine deities, rather than regular humans. A celebrity is simply a well-known person. In spiritual terms, fame means nothing. God does not care if we are famous. God cares if we follow our paths or not. Celebrities are no better than your regular Jo Schmo off the street. People put them on a pedestal, but they are really in the playpen with everyone else. Humanity seems to have gone a bit mad.

The masses are hungry for 'gurus' who will feed them exactly what they want to hear, like some kind of spiritual buffet. Celebrities can potentially exacerbate this problem in some ways, by subscribing to the messages of barmy 'gurus.' It is a win-win situation for both parties. The celebrity gets told what they want to hear and the guru earns themselves a nice wad of cash.

Please do not listen to a guru purely on the basis of a celebrity endorsement. Do your research first. They could be a nut job or a fraud. Celebrities are not a beacon for the rest of us to aspire to, and nor, necessarily, are their gurus.

A commercial guru, rather than telling the truth as it stands, will offer people a buffet of alleged spiritual answers. The individuals can then dip into the buffet and choose the particular answers they are most fond of at that moment in time, like, "You are going to marry a very rich man. You are going to buy a big house in the countryside. You are on exactly the right path to achieve all your dreams." Or they might just tell you what you already know, like, "You have two dogs, one called Buster and one called Snowy. You like shopping and you rush to purchase all the bargains in the January sales. You are thinking of re-tiling your bathroom." How is that going to help you? A good spiritual teacher will talk more generally about how you live your life, your lifestyle and emotional well-being. They will not give you direct answers, such as, "You are going to get married in March," and they will tell you the blatant truth even if sometimes, you do not want to hear it.

Life on this earth is about striving towards the Divine through learning valuable lessons, making the right choices and trusting in your intuition. It is not about drinking miracle water or wearing a belt sprinkled with holy water, to boost your spiritual ranking. It will not work. The real miracles are happening every day, in small ways and you can create those miracles if you change your life for the benefit of your soul. Your first step onto your spiritual path is a miracle, healing others and listening to others with compassion is a miracle. Your life on this earth is a miracle.

Do not get me wrong, searching for spiritual answers and the quest to better ourselves and find enlightenment is admirable. Accessing our intuition and trusting that we have all the answers we could ever need is superb. Learning as we grow each day is a blessing. The search for the truth and the

Divine that lies within holds the key to true contentment and peace. However, we should endeavour to be discerning with the information we take on board. There are some pearls of wisdom to be found from those around us, but much of what is said can be from perception rather than true intuition. The deepest answers we seek lie within us. Jesus said in the Gospel of St Thomas, "Split a piece of wood and I am there. Pick up a stone and you will find me there." [5] The Divine is around us and within us. Ultimate responsibility for accessing that Divine rests on our own intuitive connection.

If you are doing some soul searching, be careful who you put your trust in and try to avoid pseudo-spirituality. Think about your lifestyle and put spirituality into practise in your day to day living, because this is where it really counts.

The exercises that conclude this chapter will help you to ascertain what questions you would like to be answered, from a spiritual perspective. They will then help you to begin to discover those answers for yourself. We are given answers as and when we need them, not in one foul swoop.

So, be patient, keep your eyes wide open to be aware of the vital signs, be accepting and be humble before the Universe or God. If you can achieve this, before you know it you will have more answers than you ever thought possible.

"If you do not practise the spirituality you preach, then how can you call yourself spiritual?"

Dawn Mellowship

---

[5] The Gospel of Thomas; The Secret Teachings Of Jesus: Four Gnostic Gospels, Saying 75, p 33, Translated by Marvin W. Meyer, First Vintage Books, 1984.

Techniques

Finding Answers

 Grab a piece of paper and a pen and make a note of all the spiritual questions that you would like answers for.

 Sit down comfortably, either on a chair, or on the floor; make sure your back is straight. Place your list in your lap facing upwards and your palms face down on top of your list.

 Breathe in slowly and deeply through your nose for a count of five and breathe out through your mouth for a count of five. Continue this process for between three and five minutes.

 As you breathe in visualise the whole room engulfed in white light and see yourself floating in that light, with nothing else around you but the pure white glow.

 As you breathe out visualise your body expanding lengthways, growing taller and taller, until your upper body reaches through the roof and into the sky.

 Breathing normally visualise your upper body travel through the sky and into space and then beyond space to a pure white light. Feel the unconditional love from that light. Bask in the feeling of having nothing but beautiful light around you. Remain like this for fifteen to thirty minutes, thinking only about the magnificence of where you are. After regular practise of this exercise, you should get some of the answers to your questions whilst you bask in the light.

 When you have finished bring yourself back to the room and note down any answers to your questions, for reference.

Practise this exercise whenever you feel you need spiritual answers.

Being Spiritual

❑   Stand or sit in front of a mirror in your house and intently stare at yourself in the mirror.

❑   Breathe in and out through your nose very slowly and deeply and as you do so, visualise yourself becoming brighter, lighter and more ethereal.

❑   Remaining focused on yourself, continue this process for three minutes. Visualise yourself becoming ever brighter and almost more translucent. See yourself becoming more beautiful and loving. As you do so, feel this love burst forth from the image you are seeing and allow that love to surround you and enter your entire body.

❑   Visualise the mirror image of you growing taller and expanding, until it comes out of the mirror and begins to fill up the whole room, engulfing you in the process. See the image glow a very bright white.

❑   When the image of you is as bright as you can get it, silently say to yourself with meaning and purpose, eleven times, "May my soul that resides within my body shine so bright that I cannot ignore it. May my soul guide my every thought and action, may I become my soul without any distraction."

❑   To finish, re-focus your eyes on yourself in the mirror, but try to always see yourself as that beautiful image. As you walk about in daily life or sit at your desk at work, or on the bus, or on the train visualise your spiritual body expanding and getting brighter and taller, reaching for the sky and beyond.

Heaven Is Not *Really* A State Of Consciousness...

...because heaven is a tangible realm

A Tall Tale

When I was a young child, I asked my mother what heaven was. My mother was a very religious woman and she told me that heaven was where the good souls went to be with God after they died. She said that it was up above the clouds and that when the religious, pious people passed away, the pearly gates would open to let them enter the realm of heaven. This sounded wonderful and magical to me. When I went to bed that night, I squeezed my eyes tightly shut and said a silent little prayer to God. It went something like this, "Please God can you take me to heaven, so that I may see where the good souls go to."

Shortly after my prayer, I drifted off to sleep. I would usually have many dreams, but they were vague and I barely remembered them. This time it was so different. I felt myself leave my own body. First the legs, then the arms, followed by the rest of me. I looked down on myself as I slept soundly. I was floating around my bedroom. It felt so wonderful to be without the restrictions of my physical human body. I floated down the stairs and out into the middle of our back garden. It was raining heavily. I looked up above and said, "I am ready now God. Please show me heaven."

At that moment I felt myself being drawn upwards. As I ascended, I felt all my worries vanish. I was only a child but I always felt sad, this feeling just dissipated. There were no pearly gates. There was no white bearded man, but in a flash I was enveloped in this glorious white light, so bright that I could barely look at it. I felt an overwhelming sense of love and peace. I felt God all around me. I felt only this. I asked God if I could stay there but I heard a voice in my head saying, "You must go back to the earth now, you have much to do." I felt myself floating back down to the garden and into the house.

Suddenly I woke up, bolt upright in my bed. I felt incredibly hot and had this astonishing sense that something very real had happened. I could re-call my experience vividly. I knew in my heart that it had genuinely taken place.

I never told my parents or anyone else about what happened on that night, but throughout my life I tried to recreate the same experience. Time and again I asked God if I could return to heaven, but to no avail. I could not find consolation in religion. I practised meditation for many years and I would snatch moments where I felt a wonderful sense of peace and being in the moment. I would sometimes have this feeling for days.

As an avid reader, I was drawn to books that claimed that heaven was about our state of consciousness, yet this did not sit quite right with me.

One night when I went to sleep I had another vivid dream, but this time about the future of the Universe, about what would happen to our souls. I woke up with this feeling that heaven could only be attained in a real sense once our time on earth is finished, if we have made the choices that lead us there.

The heaven we can capture on this earth is a sense of inner peace, but at the same time we have to operate in a human body and be in a state of mind where we can follow our paths on this earth, to complete our work. Any type of heaven we may experience on earth cannot compare to the heaven that awaits those who will arrive there in time.

Seriously Though...

Belinda Carlisle once said that, "Heaven is a place on earth." Well if this is heaven we are in a sorry state of affairs. Heaven did not turn out to be so sublime after all. We all know that earth is not heaven, but it has been suggested that heaven is our own consciousness in its most perfect state. The earth in contrast is just the reality of our physical bodies. Heaven, it has been explained, is not a place of salvation in our future. It is the dawning on us that only the current moment we are in can free us, by the disbanding of our thoughts and ego in favour of rousing our consciousness. If heaven is not within us now, then it is but a thought with no realisation.

The example has been cited of Jesus, proclaiming to his disciples, "Heaven is right here in the midst of you." [6] Heaven, in this sense, has been described as being without ego, the 'I' or self of any individual, distinguished by their thoughts. Our surroundings may never change for the better, but heaven can be found in our own state of consciousness, or state of being. We can all attain heaven by a transition in our consciousness, attaining enlightenment, abandoning our egos.

I can perceive some truth in this belief, in that by connecting to our Divine nature within we are experiencing a glimpse of heaven. We can acquire a brief taster of heaven on earth by embracing our inner Divine nature. In meditation or during healing some more enlightened individuals can snatch cursory moments of being in heaven, where their souls leave their bodies and ascend into heaven for a while. Some people who have had near death experiences have spent some time in heaven, but this is because their souls have temporarily taken leave of their bodies.

Being enlightened or connected with our souls does not mean that we are actually in heaven itself. The Kingdom of God is among us because God is everywhere and within us is a Divine spark, but heaven can only be reached when we *truly* arrive there. When our souls leave our bodies, if we have made the choices that *can* take us there, we can arrive at the place we have coined heaven. It is not a place in a human sense but it is a realm of sorts, it is the source of God, the absolute core of the omnipotent, omnipresent, omniscient

---

[6] Luke 17:21 (New Revised Standard Edition.)

energy. God is everywhere but there are different planes, if you like. Words are so inept when it comes to describing the reality of this.

We can reside close to the source of God in heaven, when our souls depart from this world, or we can be far from the source of God. Still we are within God, but yet without God because that plane of God is devoid of unconditional love. God has a place of light and a place of darkness. Living in darkness in terms of this planet, would consist of being detached from our true spiritual nature, yet still with God's unconditional love.

Living in darkness beyond this earth would be in an actual realm of God, without any unconditional love being present. Heaven on earth could be considered to be a state of consciousness where we are connected completely with our souls and know the peace and unconditional love that is born out of that connection. Heaven beyond the earth is God's centre, the nucleus of the supreme loving intelligent energy that surrounds and engulfs us.

I have heard it stated that the future is not real, but a product of our thoughts, because there are only a series of nows. In my opinion, the future does most certainly exist. It is not just in the now. The future is looking to God or the Universe. The future will and does happen. It is known by God precisely how all events will unfold and as we become more enlightened, we too are given flashes of the future, of ourselves and of the fate of the Universe.

When we are unenlightened and lack a connection with our souls, we are deficient of the ability to know the future. As our connection begins to grow through our right thoughts and right actions, as our emotional traumas become cleared away, we start to have a more profound grasp on the future. Depending on our souls' particular journeys, we have a greater or lesser knowledge of what the future has in store. Sometimes, this knowledge is predominantly about our own future, but as we move closer to a state of enlightenment that knowledge extends to the purpose of the Universe and to the future of the Universe.

If we are dedicated completely to our spiritual growth and manage to attain a state, at least close to enlightenment, we know a great deal about exactly what will happen in the future. This knowledge aids us on our paths, to do the work we are required to do, for our Divine purposes. The future is there. It is not about to disappear. We can pretend to ignore it for a time, but one day it will catch up with us as the sands of time turn.

When Jesus pronounced, "Heaven is right here in the midst of you," he did not mean that heaven was our Divine consciousness, he was referring to himself. Jesus is God incarnate, within a physical form, part of the source of God encapsulated within a human shell. To paraphrase, Jesus was stating to his disciples, "I am heaven in the midst of you. Heaven is in front of you now and it is I."

According to the Gospel of Thomas, Jesus said, "I am the light that is over all things. I am all: from me all came forth, and to me all attained. Split a piece of wood; I am there. Lift up the stone, and you will find me there." [7] Jesus is the light, Jesus is heaven and Jesus is everywhere. In the Apocryphon of John from the Nag Hammadi Library, Jesus is said to have appeared before John in his more original form and when John becomes afraid, Jesus says, "Are you not familiar with this figure? Then do not be fainthearted! I

---

[7] The Gospel of Thomas; The Secret Teachings Of Jesus: Four Gnostic Gospels, Saying 75, p 33, Translated by Marvin W. Meyer, First Vintage Books, 1984.

am with you always. I am the Father, I am the Mother, I am the Child. I am the incorruptible and undefiled one." 8 God took itself (for God has no gender) a human form within Jesus.

Many people have struggled to get their head around whether Jesus was a human being who acted as messenger from God or a Divine being. Jesus was a Divine soul within a human body, a part of God personified. His body was a regular human body, subject to the same pain, torment and fallibility, but his soul was from the very source of God.

For many centuries, people have argued about this, but what really mattered was the message of Jesus and yet so very few individuals have come to understand that message. Instead, they argue about whether he was married or not, had children, was resurrected, where he was buried or whether he was human or Divine. What he wanted us all to understand is that we do not need any religious leaders or intermediaries between ourselves and God. We can all communicate with God, through our own intuition, which, if we have a strong connection with our souls, guides us through thought.

We have thought so that we can choose whether we listen to our souls or our physical desires. Thought is not inherently bad, we made it that way. If our thought is the whisperings of our intuition, then it serves us well. Thought is infinitely precious and it is what we use for communication after we depart from this earth.

Heaven is immeasurable in any of our human terms as God is immeasurable. There is nothing, no word or concept that does or will ever, on this earth, be able to depict

---

8 The Gospel of Thomas; The Secret Teachings Of Jesus: Four Gnostic Gospels, 1:14, p 56, Translated by Marvin W. Meyer, First Vintage Books, 1984.

the reality of what heaven or what God means. To say God is perfect, superior, all powerful, all knowing, everywhere, all loving, does not do justice to the reality of God. God is all those things, but not as we understand them on a human level and so much more than we could ever imagine, even if we attain enlightenment.

The Cambridge Dictionary describes heaven as, "In some religions, the place, sometimes imagined to be in the sky, where God lives and where good people are believed to go after they die, so that they can enjoy perfect happiness." This is a terribly Christian, in the religious sense, definition of what heaven is. Along with numerous other definitions, it diminishes much more than it clarifies the issue. We should not think of heaven in these terms. The source of God is as we would call heaven but God does not dwell purely there, God is all encompassing.

The term, 'good people' is ambiguous. There are plenty of religious followers who abide by the rituals and codes and laws of their scriptures. There are some Christians who go to church every single week, pray every morning and evening and could quote any line from the Bible. The same sorts of things could be said for those from other religions, who stick rigidly to the rituals and dogmas of their religion and often to the words of their religious leaders.

First of all, religious leaders whether they are, priests, vicars, mullas, ayatollah, rabbis, or any other title you can think of, are generally speaking, no authority for the rest of us on how we should live our lives. They are human and as such, cannot wield any real authority. Only God can do that. They act as mediators but we can all talk to God directly, we do not require such mediators. They can often complicate matters, rather than illuminating them. This is not the case for all religious leaders, but many of them misinterpret their own scriptures and besides we do not need scriptures. The word of God is inscribed within us, not laid down on a tablet or inscribed on any scrolls or in a book. A religious leader is not automatically enlightened. They are just regular human beings. They act with power and authority, but God did not grant them this power and authority, humanity did. The Universe will one day take that power away from them as it will take power away from all of us.

Secondly, following a religion dogmatically does not make anyone a 'good' person. The way we live our lives is central to the journeys of our souls'. Blindly following any religion without question, is extremely unenlightened.

We become enlightened only when we return to a state of oneness with our souls and with God, when we find our own answers through our own intuition.

Some religious devotees think that because they stick to every rule of their religion that they are in God's favour. God loves us all, unconditionally. If we make good choices that concur with our intuition, we can then become closer to God and we can perceive that unconditional love. If we make choices that steer us away from our spiritual paths, although we still have that love around us, we cannot feel it because we are so detached from our souls.

Whether we follow a religious code of practise or not, has absolutely nothing to do with it. Religion, over the years, has served as more of an obstacle to enlightenment than a bolster. It has caused more war and fighting, than peace. Religion has truly lost its way.

To be honest, we would do much better without the religious interpretations of heaven because then we could look to our intuition for the truth. Although I have discussed the concept of heaven, if we think too much in terms of heaven or hell we become fearful and make choices for the wrong reasons. We need to make choices through guidance not fear. God is nothing to fear. All we need to do is live our lives by the guidance of our intuition, to cultivate the bond with our souls. If we do that, we do not need to worry about what heaven means, because we have followed our way back to the Divine.

The exercises at the end of this Chapter will help you to find, with time and dedicated practise, an inner state of resilience, faith in your intuition and inner peace. However enlightened we become on this earth, we are always subject to circumstances. Unless we withdraw ourselves completely from society, live on a mountain top with pure air and avoid all human contact, we are going to accumulate emotional traumas. Yet, we can find an inner bliss that remains, despite our external situation.

It is possible to heal the negative energies attached to our emotional traumas. I do this through Reiki. You can find other ways of doing this, ones that suit you. Once you have achieved this, although life will not become a picnic and challenges will still arise, you will not be fettered by these. Your inner faith will shine through, you will recognise the lessons to be learned and your own journey will become ever more apparent. Embrace that journey, however hard it may seem, because the beauty, lies somewhere in the struggle.

"Heaven is the home of the imperishable Light."

Dawn Mellowship

Techniques

ASK

Only use this technique once in your whole life. Before you go to bed one night, join your hands in prayer position, in front of your chest and silently say, "If it is within Divine Love and blessing, Universe please may I be taken briefly to heaven as I sleep."

If it is within the remit of your path you may experience this, or you may not. Do not get hung up on it. Just see what happens.

Absolute Faith

❑ Sit down comfortably, either in a chair, or on the floor; make sure your back is straight. Join your hands in prayer position in front of your chest, pressing your thumbs against your sternum. Focus intently on the feeling of your middle fingers touching.

❑ Breathing in and out very slowly and deeply through your nose, stay focused on your middle fingers touching for between three and ten minutes.

❑ Keeping your hands in prayer position, on your next in breath, visualise a beam of light coming down from up above, as far as the eye can see and entering the top your head.

❑   As you breathe out, visualise the light beam travelling along your neck and shoulders, down your arms and into your palms.

❑   Continue the above two processes for between three and fifteen minutes.

❑   Place your palms on either side, at the top of your chest. Silently say to yourself fifteen times, with meaning and purpose. "May I have absolute faith in myself to follow my Divine path above all else."

❑   Return your hands to prayer position in front of your chest and repeat the same statement fifteen times.

❑   When you have finished, bow with humility to the Universe. Practise this exercise at least twice a week.

Inner Peace

❑   Sit down comfortably, either on a chair, or on the floor; make sure your back is straight. Place your palms in your lap facing upwards.

❑   Let all your worries and thoughts whir around in your head for a couple of minutes. Do not try to solve them or dwell on them, but let them be. Silently say each worry to yourself, one after the other and do not think anymore about it once you have moved onto the next one.

❑   Visualise all those worries, occupying your head, weighing you down, for three minutes.

- ❑ Still retaining the visualisation, place your palms over the sides of your head, covering your temples, with your fingers resting on the top of your head. Start to breathe in and out very slowly and deeply through your nose.

- ❑ On the next out breath, as if you are lifting off a hat, raise your hands above your head. As you do so, visualise yourself lifting those worries out of your head very forcefully. If they will not budge, pull them harder. Pull them out until both your arms are straight out above your head, palms facing each other, as if you are holding a hat full of worries right above you.

- ❑ Throw your arms forward forcefully, as if you throwing your worry hat away. As you do this, silently say to yourself, with meaning and purpose, "May the Universe convert this negative energy to positive light."

- ❑ Repeat the above three stages, between three and twenty five times, depending on what you feel you need.

- ❑ Join your hands in prayer position in front of your chest, with your head bowed down. Breathe in through your nose for a count of five and out through your nose for a count of five, for two to five minutes.

- ❑ Raise your head back up to an upright position and silently say to yourself, with meaning and purpose, nine times, "May I let go of my worries to discover an inner peace. With each new day may I experience this release."

- ❑ Bow to the Universe to finish. Practise this exercise four times a week.

You Cannot Take Responsibility For Everything...

...because you are not always to blame

A Tall Tale

I always blamed myself for everything. When I was a child I remember my parents constantly screaming, "It's your fault." They would fight with each other and to make their peace, they would blame me. Once I refused to eat all of my dinner because I was feeling really unwell and my father blamed me for his poor financial situation. He said that I was bleeding the family dry.

As I grew older, I carried a huge weight around with me, it was the weight of the world. I spent hours mulling over everything in my life and how it had all been completely of my own doing. I was constantly worried and stressed and it was only a matter of time before I plunged into a deep depression. It got to the stage where I almost tried to take my own life, well not really. I could only find a bottle of multi-vitamins in the cupboard so I downed them with half a bottle of whisky. I just woke up with a monster hangover feeling even more depressed.

I just used to sit around my flat, constantly moping. I felt numb. There was no joy or love in my life, just space and emptiness. A friend came around one day and suggested that I go to see a healer that she had heard about. I was not really in the mood, but I did not have the energy to say no, so I agreed.

The following week I went along to see the healer. She had a chat with me about my life and I talked about my parents. We went through to a room where she conducted the healing. In a matter of minutes, I had drifted off into a meditative state.

Past memories started floating around in my head. I started to feel lighter as if something was being pulled out of me. Most of the memories were events that I had previously been aware of, but one was more lucid. I saw myself as a small child giving a teddy bear to my grandmother when she had cancer. The memory returned to me at that point, that she had gone into remission. A year later the cancer returned. So, I gave her another teddy bear and again she went into remission. Within another year the cancer had returned more virulently. I did not give her a teddy this time and she died.

It suddenly occurred to me that for all these years I had blamed myself for the death of my grandmother, because I had not given her a teddy bear on her third bout of cancer.

With the realisation of this came an incredible release. I felt as if I had been set free. I had taken responsibility for everything that had happened to me in my life and suddenly I became aware that we cannot take responsibility for all our experiences, because sometimes we are not to blame.

The healing totally changed my life and now I have a balance between accepting responsibility where it is mine and abandoning it where it is not. I am so much happier as a result.

Seriously Though...

Taking responsibility for ourselves is a necessity. As human beings, we often like to shirk our responsibilities or pretend that they do not exist at all, but they are there, whether we choose to acknowledge or ignore them. If we cannot take responsibility for our actions, we will never grow and evolve spiritually. If we permanently play the victim card we deprive ourselves of self-development and we come to act incredibly irresponsibly.

We all have choices to make in life and we have to take responsibility for those choices. If we choose the option that tears us away from our own personal growth, we have to accept that we had a level of culpability. If we are impervious to our responsibilities, we tread a very physical path that is controlled by our physical desires. We wallow in self-pity and we blame others all the time, or the state of the world, or anything but ourselves. We very selfishly hurt those around us, because we do not perceive how our actions can possibly impinge on them or affect them in any way. We become very inward looking, rather than seeing the bigger picture.

If we remain in this state of being, we can potentially bring ourselves to do anything, no matter how grave, because we can shelter under our umbrella of no responsibility. "It was not my fault," we declare to ourselves and carry on our negative patterns of behaviour regardless. Our dogged refusal to take responsibility prevents us from learning from life's lessons. We lose our connection, thus we lose ourselves.

With that said, there are levels of responsibility. It is equally essential that we understand where responsibility lies with us and where it rests with others.

There are people who carry the burdens of the world upon their tired shoulders. They believe that everything that has happened in their lives and sometimes in the entire world is in some way down to them. They too wallow, but they wallow in their burden of responsibility. They say, "It is *all* my fault. Everything would be better; the world would be a better place, if it were not for me." They not only take on their own responsibilities, but everyone else's. They can then end up locked in a cycle of perpetual guilt, running around trying to mop up the pieces, running around after everyone else.

Eventually, they forget that they have truly forgotten themselves. They do not remember who they really are and they do not even realise it. Their souls plead for help because they can no longer bear the weary load. This is a huge ball and chain to drag around, a burdensome weight to rest on the shoulders of one person. Rest assured that responsibility can be shared.

There have been times in my life when I shouldered no responsibility. I loathed humankind and myself for being part of it. I eventually transcended this phase and replaced it with its antithesis, blaming my lone self for every occurrence in my life. The former phase was a very disconnected one. By the latter phase I had restored my connection but inhibited my growth with my constant self-reproach. I scoured for the deeper significance in every little circumstance. My memory played my history over and over again, on a never ending loop. What could I have done differently? How could I have shaped my future for the better? What if I had done this instead or what if I had done that instead? Why did I do those things? Why did I not know then what I had come to know now?

In time, I realised that the burden of responsibility was a composite one, that some of the blame rested with me and some with those around me. I needed to accept the responsibility that was mine and concede the rest. Once I had accepted responsibility where it was due, I needed to let go of the past and the guilt, accept that I had learned from my experiences and gracefully move on.

I also discovered that some events happen without a greater significance for me than that they took place. They would have happened a certain way regardless of my actions and dwelling on them was futile, because it was stifling my spiritual development. We like to delve for meanings in every little happening, but sometimes there are none to be found. Our actions would not have altered the consequences. There was nothing we could do. Perhaps the lesson was not for us but for someone else and there is nothing for us to gain from it. To accept this, is a fantastic release. It can set you free from the shackles, the cross that you bear. The past becomes a memory because you are no longer there. Time unfolds as it should.

Our degree of personal responsibility depends on our understanding and awareness at the time in question, along with the circumstances surrounding our life experiences. As our understanding and awareness increases throughout our lives, so too does our level of responsibility. The older we become, the more we are responsible for our actions in life. As we grow from children into adults we, hopefully, develop more understanding and awareness. This awareness brings with it greater responsibility.

In ignorance we have far less responsibility because we are unaware of the consequences of our actions. When I say ignorance, I mean *true* ignorance. There are many who plead ignorance when they are really aware, but they choose to live in a permanent state of denial. Feigning ignorance does not absolve anyone of their responsibilities. In fact, it adds extra responsibilities because we have to face the reality that we know far more than we are letting on. If deep down we know something is wrong for us, but we act as if we do not know, we are only lying to ourselves. Our souls and the Universe cannot be duped.

If, for example, we develop an illness but try to pass the responsibility onto others or God, we are doing ourselves a great disservice. An illness is often an opportunity for us to learn and to develop. The contributing causes can frequently be traced to our lifestyle choices and as a result of stress and emotional traumas.

Rather than pleading ignorance, we need to accept that we are being given an invaluable opportunity to re-assess our lifestyles and make the appropriate choices for the future. Sometimes, the lessons are not purely for us and they help those around us, such as our families and friends. It might not seem very helpful at the time, but in reality it can foster our strength, if we choose to learn from it.

If an individual passes away from an illness, or lives in a conscious and healthy way, but still becomes chronically sick, the lesson may not just be for them but for the people around them. In some cases, it may be *solely* for the people around the ill individual and not the afflicted person. If we choose to see everything as a lesson rather than a bugbear life becomes more of a blessing. We also have to remember that some things are just beyond our control, which I will discuss later on.

The more enlightened and aware we become, the more responsibility we have, the more we fully understand the implications of our choices and actions. This is why in a high state of awareness and enlightenment we can, in a sense, do less. The more we know, the less we can do in terms of our physical desires and path because we are aware enough to know that these things are not conducive to our spiritual growth. For instance, once you accept that all animals are living, sentient beings with a soul, you cannot bring yourself to eat them. Once you realise that your spiritual path is the key to all life, you cannot do anything that would in any way compromise your spiritual journey. Your awareness and level of intuition would be too immense to revert backwards to a desire driven lifestyle.

As your awareness develops, your soul takes control of your physical and emotional bodies and that includes your ego.

I would like to talk more about our levels of personal responsibility. This is an emotive subject but also a very important one. You will probably have a set series of beliefs on this already and they may not corroborate with what I have to say, but it is a complex, multi-faceted area and I can only skim the surface. The more complicated and grave the actions are; the more formidable ascertaining levels of responsibility becomes.

A child that was abused by an adult in some way, shape or form can bear no responsibility for their suffering. The responsibility rests entirely with the offending adult.

A child that becomes obese due to poor nutrition has learned their pattern of behaviour from their parents or guardians. Thus, their parents or guardians must bear the responsibility for the child's state of being.

However, if the abused child grows up to be a very abusive adult, the entire situation becomes decidedly more complex. Their level of responsibility is not quite so simple to decipher. It will depend on factors such as how aware they are and what their state of mind is like. If they were abused so consistently that they have become highly psychologically damaged because of it, if abuse and aggression is all they have ever known, it becomes incredibly awkward to ascertain their precise degree of culpability.

I would say though, that if the abuser knows that what they are doing is wrong, if they have a feeling that their actions are erroneous, they have a significantly greater level of responsibility. They know that what they are doing is wrong, but they are choosing to ignore their innate intuition.

Children have some level of personal responsibility. If a child strolls into the school playground and proceeds to stab another child with a knife, they may have a degree of responsibility for their actions. Again this will depend on their state of mind, level of awareness, the circumstances of the event and their upbringing. It is highly probable that the parents would wield a large portion of the responsibility, but without knowing the exact circumstances of the event we cannot be completely sure of this. We have to look at each individual situation on its merits.

You can take the entire realm of responsibility to extremes. Society is interwoven and sometimes puzzling. We can tend to view our different cultures and societies as being heterogenous, but in some ways we are more homogenous than we like to think. We are different in the flesh, in our cultures, languages and beliefs. Our souls all have different journeys and paths, but humans are constructed from the same source. Our energy fields are constantly interacting with others and our actions affect more people than we would often dare to realise. We each have one finger pressed against a domino. If we constantly act against our intuition and flout our responsibilities we could topple all the other dominos, set off a chain reaction and get more trouble than we bargained for.

Returning to my original point, we are all conditioned by society. Society informs our sense of who we are and what the world is about. Our societies and cultures play a part in the choices we make and in our actions. Sometimes, assessing degrees of responsibility is clearer cut, but at other times it is much more interwoven into the fabric of society. You could have promiscuous sex, feel remorseful and then blame the state of our culture, the way in which women are viewed as sex objects, this being thoroughly exacerbated by the media, modelling and music industries. You could plough your way through history citing how women have historically been perceived as the weaker sex, with assigned roles. Where do we draw the line?

We need to be realistic with our responsibilities and careful not to blame all our misdemeanours on the condition of the planet. Regardless of what is going on around us, we have our own insight and intuition. Of course, all of this is a huge factor in our growth and development, but most of us come to a point where we are aware enough to make the right choices.

Each one of us has an innate sense of the laws of the Universe, at least at some point during our lives. Despite what life throws at us, most of us will reach a stage in our lives when we become aware of the differences between right and wrong. This is not so much a moral compass because morality can be fed by our conditioning. It is the congenital calling of our intuition, the voices of our souls. We might kid ourselves that we do not know any better, but if we were to be perfectly honest with ourselves, most of us would realise that we really do.

As babies and very young children our parents are responsible for nurturing us, fostering our well-being and personal development. As we progress out of this stage to our adolescent years, we become increasingly responsible for our own behaviour and in adulthood even more so.

Whilst our environment, upbringing and conditioning form our sense of ourselves and the Universe to a degree, we still ultimately hold responsibility for many of our actions. This can be perceived in the consequences that find their way into our laps. If you are wondering why life seems so tough, think about how your own actions may have contributed to those consequences.

Our experiences are highly complex and the cases in our lives where responsibilities are perfectly clear cut tend to be scant. More often than not, we need to take into account the actions of all those surrounding us as well as ourselves. We need to accept where the responsibility rested with us and where it rested elsewhere. With who does not matter, as long as we take what it ours and relinquish the rest. If we cannot fathom precisely with whom responsibility was due because of complexities, as long as we can wholeheartedly accept that we did have some responsibility, as long as we can learn from our errors, we can move on.

We need to accept the guilt that is due to us as a result of our negative actions, learn from our mistakes and then carry on with our lives in a considerably more conscious manner. Do not forget the past completely. It serves as a reminder of where you came from, of what you have learned. Your past helps you to help others. It reminds you of the journey you have taken. Yet, do not dwell always on the past because it is dead and buried and you should be looking to how you can improve your life in the present and the future. Be kind to yourself and gentle with yourself. Learn from the course of your life, but be careful not to asperse judgement on it. Judgement is for the Universe.

Poor Old Guilt

Talking about guilt in that last paragraph, I have to say that guilt gets a rough deal. Some people believe in vanquishing all guilt, but we do actually need guilt to a point. If we felt no guilt we would feel no remorse for our actions. We need to live with our guilt until we have learned from our mistakes, then we should let our guilt go. If we have not learned from our mistakes and we are continuing the same old negative patterns of behaviour, then guilt stays with us, to indicate that we are pursuing the wrong path.

We have to be honest with ourselves and not feign a transformation, when in reality; we are following the same old vicious cycle. We may temporarily fool ourselves and even others, but our souls and God knows us in our entirety. It does not matter how bad our actions have been, if we are truly repentant and we turn to our spiritual path, happiness and peace can be ours.

A murderer can discover their way to enlightenment if they change their life and pursue their soul path. Another individual might not have undertaken anything so drastic, but throughout their life followed the course of their physical desires and deliberately, never once looked to their spiritual needs. In this case, the murderer could reach enlightenment and experience the unconditional love of being with God, whilst the other individual may possibly never experience that feeling. This is because the former person chose to walk their spiritual path, no matter how tiny the footsteps, but the latter chose to flagrantly ignore their spiritual needs.

In this particular incidence, the murderer has taken complete responsibility for their actions and moved on. The other individual has chosen to avoid their responsibilities and both will have crafted a certain chain of consequences as a result of their actions in life. One set of consequences leads to the Divine, the other away from it.

It does not matter what we have done in our lives, how atrocious it may seem, as long as we find our way back to our Divine paths and follow the guidance of our intuition, we can discover unconditional love and happiness.

It Was Not Meant For You

I explained earlier that some events just happen and nothing we can do would have changed anything. Some things that happen in life are totally beyond our control. It is a waste of time trying to apportion responsibility in such cases because whatever choice you had made would have resulted in the same consequence. Whatever the particular experience was, it may not have been a lesson for you to learn. Sometimes, the lesson is for others who were involved in the incidence.

Someone may have followed their spiritual path all of their life and then someone walked up to them in the street at random and punched them on the chin, for what appears to be no reason whatsoever, that they can conceive of. There was nothing they could do about it. The victim may well wish that they had not passed down the street on that particular occasion, but for all we know, the incident could have taken place anywhere. If the person had not lived a spiritual path, it may still have happened. If they had lived somewhere else, it may still have occurred. That clout around the chops may well be a lesson for the perpetrator and not the victim. I have given a pretty crude example, but you get the idea. If you are constantly ruminating about something that happened to you that you cannot decipher, then it may be time to let that incident go. If your intuition can make no headway, the lesson could well be for someone else.

As you can imagine, responsibility is a challenging area, but we should try to take responsibility for our actions. We can choose to learn from the past and take steps towards our personal growth. The more aware you become, through spiritual development, the more responsibility you will be given. It might sound like a hell of a chore, but it really is not. In fact you can find yourself clamouring to be given more responsibility because it is so very rewarding.

The exercises at the end of this chapter will help you to start taking responsibility for yourself, to surrender the accountability that is not yours and hopefully, to let go of any guilt and move forward. When you can finally achieve this, you will find yourself in a much more beautiful and happy place. To accept responsibility and in turn, to leave the guilt behind, is a wonderful experience to be cherished. It signifies a critical milestone in your journey towards self-development and spiritual growth.

This will not be an overnight process. We spend our entire lives accruing inner feelings of guilt and self-loathing. Punishing ourselves is something we have become familiar with.

For those who believe in God, God does not want us to punish ourselves. Some people, especially certain religious followers, believe that by indulging in self-punishment they can become closer to God. Some people believe that Jesus' suffering on the cross was an indication to humanity that we should inflict punishment on ourselves. This is utter twaddle. God wants us to cherish, love and nurture ourselves. We do not become closer to God by self-punishment. We become closer to God by thinking and living in the right way. This amounts to following our intuitive guidance.

"It is easy to dodge our responsibilities, but we cannot dodge the consequences of dodging our responsibilities."

Josiah Charles Stamp

Techniques

Releasing

 Sit down comfortably, either on a chair, or on the floor; make sure your back is straight. Place your palms in your lap facing upwards.

 Breathing normally visualise a waterfall of white light coming down from up above, as far as the eye can see and entering the top of your head. Push the light down your neck, down your entire chest and stomach to your tanden (3cm below your navel on the inside of your body.)

 Maintaining the visualisation above, see the light in your navel area forming into a giant globe of white light. Each time you breathe out the globe gets bigger and brighter.

 Visualise the globe rotating rapidly like a big round vortex and hear it whirring. As it rotates faster and faster, see the white vortex sucking in black negative energy from your body. Feel it sucking out the negative energy from every little crook and cranny: your feet, legs, back, stomach, arms, head, neck, organs, brain and so on.

 Continue this process for three to fifteen minutes. When you feel that the light can suck in no more, on your next out breath, forcefully push the globe vortex, with all that negative energy, out of the front of your body and send it spinning off into the Universe.

 Silently say to yourself, with meaning and purpose, "May the Universe please convert this negative energy to positive light."

Practise this exercise as often as you can.

Understanding Responsibility

❑   Lie down comfortably on your back, either on a sofa, the floor or your bed, with your arms resting by your sides, palms facing upwards. Close your eyes.

❑   Think of an emotionally traumatic experience from your life and hold that memory in your head for a few moments.

❑   Visualise a rainbow (with the colours red, orange, yellow, green, blue, indigo, violet); sprouting from the centre of your forehead, and moving down in a semi-circle, so the end of the rainbow comes to rest on the tips of your toes. You should in effect have a rainbow covering you from head to toe.

❑   Breathe in and out very slowly and deeply through your nose, feeling your stomach and chest rise, as you breathe in and fall as you breathe out. As you do this, retain the visualisation of the rainbow. It should almost be as if you can see a portion of the rainbow above your eyes. You do not have to constantly focus on the entire rainbow (from a point outside of your body), but rather the part of the rainbow that is above your head. See the colours growing brighter and brighter. Retain this visualisation for between three and ten minutes.

❑   Bring your mind back to your memory and keep that memory in the centre of your forehead, for a moment. On your next out breath, push an image of the memory (as if it is on a television or cinema screen) along the rainbow, so it travels from your head to your feet.

- ❏ Still visualising the memory at the base of the rainbow, silently say to yourself, with meaning and purpose, seven times, "May the Universe allow me to see, what part of this memory is my responsibility. May I abandon the rest, which does not belong to me."

- ❏ Visualise the memory at the end of the rainbow dissipating and becoming more translucent, until you can only see the rainbow.

- ❏ Silently, say to yourself, with meaning and purpose, "May this knowledge come to me when I need it. I let it go until I receive it."

- ❏ Visualise the two ends of the rainbow bending upwards so that the rainbow becomes a horizontal beam floating above your body. See the rainbow float down into your body, keeping it there, gently open your eyes.

From regular practise of this technique, you should eventually be able to establish where responsibility lies for that particular memory and it will help you to then let it go. Keep practising this same technique for each memory, until you feel intuitively that you have dealt with that experience, then move onto another experience from your life.

Give The Ego A Break...

...because it is a part of who you are

A Tall Tale

I used to be a dope-head, sitting around doing nothing with my mates and getting high. A few years ago, I started to think about the way I was living my life. I never really felt satisfied, no matter what I did in life. I craved attention and sought solace in my addiction. I was always the one who made my friends laugh. I felt like they expected it from me. I felt like I was who they wanted me to be and I did not know who I *really* was.

This dilemma led me to attend a spiritual workshop. I was hoping to find some kind of peace of mind. Above all, I thought I might discover a better sense of myself. I became tired of being a bum. It might have been fun for a while, but my head was always up in the clouds and the world seemed imaginary.

The spiritual workshop focused very much on us letting go of our ego. The teacher encouraged us to embrace the here and now, to let go of our thoughts and to just be. This is the fundamental message that I took home with me after the workshop and I decided to put it into action.

I sat on the sofa for days, just being, or trying to be anyway. I tried to feel the state I was in, my emotional state of mind, without dwelling on those emotions. I sat and sat and sat, until a week had passed. I felt totally detached from my human existence. I felt a space around me. I had barely eaten and I had not brushed my teeth or even bothered to shave. I did not see the point. During those days, I had felt more at peace. I drifted in and out of consciousness.

On the seventh day, I sat up and thought to myself, "What the hell am I doing? I have been sat on my backside all week doing absolutely nothing." I realised that this is what I had being doing before, but this time I was doing it with an apparently more legitimate excuse. I was becoming much more aware in one sense, but in another I was ignoring my purpose.

For ages after that realisation I slipped back into my usual old ways, disappointed that my ego had not suddenly evaporated. Then one day, I just decided to get up and do something. I had a thought that popped into my head from that previous experience. I suddenly realised that fooling myself I would be devoid of all ego was giving me a license to shirk responsibility. I did not have to *do* anything. I could just *be* and the rest would automatically be taken care of. I realised that my thoughts were of incredible value.

I smoked my last spliff to remind me of the old days and set about changing my life. After all, being in a physical body I had personal responsibilities. I went out and got a job, I learned to trust my intuition and I made positive choices in life. My thoughts did not stop, quite the contrary, rather they were propelling me in the right direction. I bought myself a decent flat and everything I could ever possibly need to live a fairly comfortable lifestyle.

I did not feel dominated by my possessions. I did not feel they gave me a sense of who I was. This came from my inner intuitive self and to a lesser extent from my physical and emotional bodies. I still very much enjoyed some of the same things I had done previously, just not the ones that were harmful to my personal development. I felt that I was growing spiritually, without vanquishing my ego. I found this to be a truly happy balance.

In that week where I had just sat around 'being' I was too detached from my external reality. I was trying too hard to rid myself of something that I needed to operate in this world. I finally decided to give my ego a break, because it is really, part of who I am. It is my sense of self.

Seriously Though...

Poor old ego, it always takes a battering from the self-help brigade. "Do away with the ego," they say, "Your ego is your sense of your self, based on your thinking mind. Let it go." I have even had a bit of a bash at the ego myself in the past, well mammoth egos anyway. This is because gigantic egos, dominated purely by our physical and emotional desires are a big mistake. Being controlled by pure ego is a complete recipe for disaster in terms of the journeys of our souls. If we are dominated by our ego alone, we forget about listening to our intuition and base all our physical and emotional desires and our entire sense of ourselves, in the terms of our culture, our environment and our conditioning.

However, ego does not have to be such a terrible thing. I am going to stamp my foot down petulantly and stand in the corner of the ring mopping ego's brow and giving it a pep talk before the match. In simple terms, as I know no other, we would all be vegetative without our egos. We would lounge around blob like on the sofa, staring into space vacantly. To clarify this, I am going to illuminate a couple of common interpretations of the ego and then disclose my own theory on this concept. If I am to be perfectly honest, I do not see why we even *need* the word ego. There are other ways to explain our sense of ourselves, which I will explain later on.

The word ego is drawn from the Latin and translates into "I myself." Many of us have come to recognise ego as the Freudian concept. The Ego, Id and Super-ego portray the divisions between the unconscious and conscious minds. Our Id represents our primitive physical drives or our instincts, specifically in terms of our sexual 'instincts.' The Ego handles all of our external realities, arbitrating between the primitive instincts of our Id and the reality of our physical and social environments.

In his early work Freud discussed the Ego in terms of our sense of self, but he later came to depict it more in terms of our psychological functions.

The Super-Ego is a sense of conscience, created by an association with the father figure, as the young boy cannot possess his own mother sexually, for fear of being castrated. Women were already perceived as being castrated by Freud because they had weak Super-Egos. It follows The Oedipus Complex, a stage in the child's development where children view their own fathers as adversaries, competing for the sole possession of their mothers' love.

I know, it sounds nuts doesn't it? I am not a big fan of Freud's suppositions. Much of Sigmund Freud's work has been discredited. I perceive Freud's theories as misogynistic and he was so enlightened that he declared cocaine to be a "magical drug."

The ego has also been examined in more spiritual terms. It is viewed as an obstacle to achieving enlightenment. According to such theories, it creates a disparity between us when we are in reality truly at one. The ego is, in these terms, a sense of the self based on conditioning and environment. It is an artificial self, crafted by an unconscious affiliation with the mind.

The ego, it is believed by some, is obsessed with time and persistently thinks to guarantee its future existence. This prevents us from being in the present because we are always looking to the past and future and this in turn allows our egos to retain their supremacy. Peace and Nirvana spell the complete end of the ego and so the ego tries to prevent us experiencing this reality.

To me, this concept of the ego really lacks something. It blithely forgets that we are in a physical world and have to operate in physical, flesh and bone, exceedingly real, bodies. It lacks enlightened *thought*. Maybe I am missing something here, but I will now give you my ten pence worth, for all *it* is worth.

Before I delve into the labyrinth of the ego, I am going to explain something without even using this notorious term. We each have a physical, emotional and spiritual body. The way I see it, we can be dominated purely by our physical desires, purely by our emotional wants, we can be dominated by a mixture of the two or we can we dominated by our physical, our emotional and our spiritual bodies, with our spiritual bodies guiding the other two. The latter of these is the ideal. Both our physical and emotional bodies should act in accordance with our intuition. This does not mean that they have no sense of self in physical or emotional terms, but that this sense of self is informed by intuition and to a lesser degree, by the other two bodies. Enlightenment is not the banishment of the thinking mind. We were granted thought for a purpose, but rather enlightenment is when thoughts follow intuition. Our thoughts are indispensable because our souls communicate with us via these channels. The sense of self is intuitive, but we function in physical bodies, on earth and this too informs our sense of self, but in a much more enlightened way.

Now I will bring in the ego as a sense of self. The sense of who you are derives from your physical existence, your emotional perception and well-being and your spiritual connection. If the sense of yourself comes purely from your physical existence, then your ego (or sense of self) will be based entirely on all your physical achievements and the procurement of your physical desires. You will gather your sense of self from what you have in physical terms, by the accumulation of products, money, power, sexual prowess, status and such like.

If your physical body exists without input from the other two, you will objectify other people and perhaps even yourself. We are witnessing in our popular culture, with the propagation of the sexualisation of advertising and the media, that people are creating their identity and sexuality based on people as objects. Children are receiving their sex education from the television and this teaches a very detached sexuality. It promotes the accumulation of possessions to make us better people. We are being shown that if you slap on the right aftershave, perfume, and beauty products and adorn the in vogue designer clothes, this makes you a happier, worthier and sexier individual.

We have come to judge each other by what we have and what we wear and that gives us our sense of self. This is vital to capitalism, as it has come to pass, because confusing our status and sense of identity with purchasing products keeps us queuing up in the shopping aisles. Thus, by virtue of how the world has come to be, there are many people driven solely by their physical desires.

If your sense of yourself springs purely from your emotional body, then you define who you are by your emotional conditioning, your environment and within, from negative energy left within your body from past emotional traumas. You will gather your sense of self from how you are perceived by others and will most likely seek their constant approval and recognition. We see this happening a lot with celebrities. They judge themselves by their fame and level of adulation from their fans. If they lose their fame, they feel lost and distraught because their sense of who they are came from how others looked upon them.

If we are dominated by our emotional bodies we become obsessed with conditional love and approval. We torment ourselves constantly, thinking, "Why don't they like me? I wish they would like me. What can I do to make them like me?" We become slaves to our emotions and they shoot off all over the place in phases of depression, irrational anger, irrational fear, jealousy, resentment, apathy, sadness and brief episodes of pleasure, but never genuine happiness.

If your sense of self emanates from your physical and emotional bodies, you will define yourself by a combination of your physical successes and your emotional conditioning. You will label yourself according to objects and approval. Do you have the right status, products and level of power and do you have the approval of your peers and other people? You will look for both because they will bolster your sense of who you are as an individual.

If your sense of yourself originates purely from your spiritual body, it will mean that you are ignoring the reality of your life and failing to execute your earthbound duties. You are ignoring a big part of yourself and pretending that it does not exist, rather than dealing with it. We have souls but we are here on earth, in physical bodies, experiencing a physical life and we have to accept this and deal with it. It can seem easier to dismiss the real world, the truth of that world and to retreat into a shell. But by doing this, we try to see the world as we wish it would be, rather than how it really is. We ignore the pain and struggle that is a part of this world. We view all our suffering as entirely self-inflicted because it is easier to digest, so that we may sink into our safe asylum, rather than accepting that our suffering is also caused by others. We fail to take the action that our souls depend on.

If we retreat entirely into our spiritual bodies, we are merely suppressing the other two, suppressing the ego, but it has not disappeared and will create conflict within us, even if we are not aware of it.

You may be directed by your physical and emotional bodies with momentary influences from your spiritual body, where the intuitive connection is there, but not strong. In this case, you will mostly pursue the self-destructive and perhaps even externally destructive instructions of your physical and emotional bodies, with rare glimpses of insight from your intuition. Sometimes, you will take the right course of action, listening to your inner wisdom, but on many other occasions you will be pulled in conflicting directions, confused by the somewhat contradictory messages emerging from your three divergent bodies.

You, indeed we, need to have balance. Your sense of self needs to originate from all three bodies, but your spiritual body, your intuition, should be guiding your physical and emotional existence. Then, you will follow your higher path on earth, listen to your intuition intently and you will know your soul completely, but recognising that your soul inhabits a physical body that incorporates thought; that incorporates emotion.

Some self-help experts and self-proclaimed spiritual teachers have ridden roughshod over poor old thinking, but we have thought for a reason and thought does not need to be disbanded, but guided by our intuition. Our emotions too, can be guided by our higher selves.

When you become enlightened, you do not lose who you are in a physical and emotional sense. Your physical and emotional bodies elevate to a more Divine level and fall more into line with your spiritual body. You are still **you**, which could be, the person that laughs at others misfortunes, the person who enjoys watching the football, the person who likes watching television programmes about being the next top model and the person who likes to wear nice clothes and work out hard at the gym. You will leave behind some other elements of your physical and emotional bodies that were damaging to your spiritual path. For instance, I gave up drinking alcohol, smoking and eating animal products, because these things were detrimental to my spiritual path. However, I retained other aspects of my character. I still have an ego, but it is guided by my intuition.

You really do not need to relinquish every part of your thinking mind. It *does* form who you are on earth, but if it is guided by your spiritual body, it will act according to your spiritual path. You are still, most likely, going to buy products, in order to live comfortably, but they will not dominate your entire existence, or act as a means of defining yourself. You might still like buying nice stuff, but it will not be your personal measure of your success and identity; that will come instead from your spiritual connection. You are not going to fall into the depths of despair if you do not get everything you want in life, because you will have the wisdom to want what you need.

You can still sit in front of the television and watch adverts and you will probably still get the jingles lodged in your brain, but you will be in a place of awareness, enabling you to detach yourself from the attempted indoctrination. Your thoughts will not cease to exist; they will just become more Divine thoughts. My intuition communicates with me through the medium of thought. This is very common. So, I say, leave poor thought alone!

Back to our good old friend ego; ego, or our sense of self, is not inherently a bad thing if it is lead by our spiritual bodies, with our other bodies following, in terms of how we tread our paths. Ego is only bad when it is controlled purely by our physical, emotional or physical *and* emotional bodies. Then it searches for the wrong kind of satisfaction, rather than falling into line with our intuition.

I have heard it said that our ego is not who we really are. It stifles our state of just being, which is who we really are. I say that whatever and whoever you are, is what and who you have become. It might not be what your soul is, but it is who **you** are in terms of your earthly existence.

In the past, I got to a point where I had completely disconnected from my poor soul and intuition because of the reckless way I was living my life. I destroyed my connection and became controlled by something much darker. I am not now going to say, that was not me. It would seem easy and safe to do that. I could say then, "Oh well I could not help it, it was my anger, or my bad old ego controlling me." Without lowering the tone to expletives, I have to say, hogwash. I accept my responsibility. Some of it was mine, some of it was down to others, but fundamentally that was who *I* was. That was me. It was not a distortion of reality. It was who I had turned myself into. The only way out of that was to establish my intuitive connection and intrinsically, change who I had become, and take action. The person I was before was not my soul, but she was me, at that time. She was my earthly representation.

If I had stayed on that harmful path, I would have remained a reckless and damaged individual, toying with the dark side of human nature. Thankfully, I escaped.

Being in the moment, or being present, is not enough to expel an ego. You have to actually get up off your jacksy, do something positive and simply let your ego follow your spiritual guidance. Reiki re-connected me to my intuition, but that was not enough. I could have sat on my backside 'being,' until the cows came home, but instead I chose to put effort and conscious thought into following the right path. You can do this without losing your ego. As I have repeatedly said, like a broken record, your ego is OK, as long as you let it be governed in the right way.

Our ego also motivates us to do some essential things in life. We would not take care of ourselves if it were not for our ego. Not everything we absorb from our conditioning is bad. One up for the ego!

When our souls take leave from our bodies at our very final destinations and become pure energy we still have a sense of who we are, but without experiencing this through our physical and our emotional bodies, as we do on earth. We experience this as energies. Until we reach this point, we cannot know how this would feel, because we are so tied into our mortal, human lives. The term ego then, will be entirely meaningless, because words are the medium we utilise for communication on earth, but this is not so in our energy forms.

As usual I have included some exercises for you, should you wish to undertake them. These techniques, if practised regularly enough, will help your ego to be guided by your intuitive voice rather than solely by your physical and emotional bodies. You can, at times, temporarily disconnect from your physical and emotional bodies, during meditation, healing or other moments of stillness. However, you cannot permanently remain in this state because the nature of the world and the paths of our souls, require that we engage in thoughts and actions. Thoughts are intrinsic to our journeys on earth and beyond.

Don't beat yourself up for not being able to switch off your ego completely. Your sense of self is vital, as long as it is being predominantly derived from the most evolved part of you, which is your soul. I am going to stop banging on about the ego now, lest you may obsess too much over it. Just listen to your intuition and act in accordance with it. If you do this, you cannot go wrong.

"Your ego is who you are. Your soul is who you should be; with your ego under its authority."

Dawn Mellowship

Techniques...

Intuitive Ego

 Sit down comfortably, either on a chair, or on the floor; make sure your back is straight. Place your palms in your lap, facing upwards.

 Breathe in and out slowly through your nose, counting to five on each in breath and counting to five on each out breath. Continue this process for three minutes.

 Join your hands in prayer position, in front of your chest.

 Breathe in through your nose very slowly and on your next out breath make a "*Haa*" sound with your mouth, pushing it out from your stomach. Continue this process for between three and five minutes.

 Silently say to yourself, with meaning and purpose, seven times, "May my intuition guide my ego, so that where my intuition goes, my ego follows."

 Repeat the above two steps, three times.

 Bow to the Universe to finish.

Practise this exercise three times a week.

Identifying A Negative Ego

❑ Grab yourself a piece of pen and some paper for this exercise. Write a list of personal traits you have, that you feel could be considered as negative ego. It does not matter whether anyone else thinks they are. It is what **you** think that matters. This might, for instance, include characteristics such as: seeking the approval of others, coveting material goods, manipulating other people to get what you want etc.

❑ When you have finished, write down what you feel is good about your ego. This could be your wicked sense of humour, your motivation to look after yourself; being caring, nurturing and sensitive etc.

❑ Sit down comfortably, either on a chair, or on the floor; make sure your back is straight. Place your list in your lap and place your left palm on the list of your positive ego traits and your right palm on the list of your negative ego traits.

❑ As you breathe in through your nose, very slowly and deeply, silently say to yourself, with meaning and purpose, five times, "My intuition guides me to accomplish my positive ego."

❑ As you breathe out through your mouth, very gently, silently say to yourself, with meaning and purpose, five times, "My intuition replaces my negative ego."

❑ Repeat the above two processes five times.

❑ Removing your hands from the lists, join them in prayer position, in front of your chest, focusing on the feeling of your middle fingers pressed against each other. Breathing very slowly and deeply, through your nose. Continue this process for between three and five minutes.

❑ Bow to the Universe to finish.

Once you have completed the exercise, have another look at your list and see if you have anything to add or subtract from any of the sections. As you practise this technique over time, keep going back to your list and you should hopefully be adding more traits to the positive ego section and eliminating the negative ego traits, step by step.

With time and effort, you can reach a point, where you have achieved a purely positive ego and dissolved the negative ego.

When you get to this point, you are being governed by your intuition to a much greater extent. As you grow and develop spiritually, if you move far and fast enough along your spiritual path, your physical and emotional bodies will be entirely governed by your intuition. Your thoughts will thus become enlightened thoughts and your ego will become beneficial, rather than harmful to you and to those around you. This is the state you should be keeping in mind and aiming for. This is enlightenment.

Time Is Of The Essence...

...because we do not have unlimited time

A Tall Tale

For most of my life, I was obsessed with time. I was always running late and my life seemed to be manic. I was not only pre-occupied with what the time was, but also with what time had come to mean for my life. The past was my homestead and the future was where my goals would be achieved. I was driving myself insane with all these pre-occupations. I forgot to look at where I was, at this moment.

Eventually, I had just had enough of living my life in this erratic way. I decided to be in each and every moment and pool all my focus into that single moment. I stopped thinking about the past and I only thought of the future for time keeping purposes. Various sources had suggested that time was an illusion and that the past was only a part of our thoughts, of our memory. The future was our expectation without realisation.

After a few months, it became very apparent that nothing was happening. I did not feel as if I had moved forward. I felt as if I had become marooned in the present. I was not becoming more enlightened. I was not even taking responsibility for myself. I was wandering upwards on a descending escalator, neither going backwards or forwards. I was not thinking at all.

A few weeks after a car accident, I started to think about the past and I realised that it was not a figment of my imagination. It was not just a thought, the past truly existed. I had been driving without a seatbelt. I did not even notice. I was not thinking. Before I knew it, I had been flung right out of the windscreen.

I was resting at home and staring at my injuries. It made me think of the accident. The scars were still there. The past occurred and I had the scars to prove it. I was not just thinking about it. It happened, not now, but in the past. I started to think about the future and instead of just relying on the now, I made plans and set realistic obtainable goals. The past entered my mind fleetingly, but only so I could learn from it.

My spiritual development soared as I spent each day meditating. With this growth, came wonderful new insights about the future. It became very apparent that I had tasks to fulfil in a set amount of time. Some things had to be done hurriedly, whilst others could wait a bit longer. I had not lost a sense of being in the present, but, at the same time I was aware of how the past and future reflected on the present. It occurred to me that time is of the essence because our time is really quite limited. The world will not last forever, nor will our bodies and in that brief moment of time we have on earth, we have much to do.

Seriously Though...

Time, really is, of the essence. The past, present and future are all extraordinarily important. Whether we think about the past or not, our past creates consequences for our present and our future and we **will** experience the consequences of our actions whether we choose to live in the now, the past or the future.

One school of thought deems the future to be a sum of our fears and dreams, a series of thoughts. When the future arrives, it will be in the form of the present time, the now. However, I posit that the future is there in front of us. It is not just a collection of thoughts. It is tangible, real and certain. We need to be highly conscious of how we live our lives, of our thoughts and actions, with a view to our future being the best it can possibly be for our paths and purposes. Time will always tell, on this earth.

It has been stated that you cannot make the state of being devoid of ego a future goal to work towards. Firstly, there is no need for us to be devoid of ego, as I discussed in the previous chapter. Secondly, it is entirely possible to have goals that will take place in the future. You can set yourself the goal of becoming enlightened in the future and then with each day, take steps towards accomplishing that goal. Each step will be rooted in your present time, but each subsequent step will be sowed in the future.

Some philosophies espouse the idea that everything takes place in the now, that nothing ever occurred in the past or in the future. Thoughts of the past are seen as memory traces of previous present moments and our thoughts of the future are seen as anticipation of what has not yet happened. However, time is a sequence and the past has footprints. If you broke your car last week and you still have not fixed it, this is not a memory trace. It actually occurred and your car still has the damage to verify that this past event took place.

Events are not memory traces. If you were blinded as a child and you remain blind as an adult, this is not your memory trace. It was an actual event that happened in the past. The famous American physicist, Albert Einstein once said that, "The only reason for time is so that everything does not happen at once." I cannot validate that this is the sole reason for time, but if everything happened in the present, surely it would all happen at once and the world as we know it could potentially have ceased to exist. Perhaps it already has!

Exact knowledge of the future may not be accessible to everyone, but anyone can gain brief glimpses of the future and the enlightened have a phenomenal awareness of what the future will bring, in terms of their own paths and of the destiny of the Universe as a whole. The future can be known. The stronger our intuitive connections are the greater our foresight is, the more we know about the future of this earth. This knowing is not a series of thoughts or musings, but an innate understanding, a profound knowledge.

Being aware and being enlightened means having foresight and foreknowledge, being thoroughly aware of the implications of the past, present *and* future.

As I said in an earlier chapter, the world is real and following on from that, time is not an illusion. It may not be relevant after we reach our final destinations, but on earth, in each life cycle, it has a very distinct purpose.

You only have to observe the beauty of nature to identify that each level of consciousness, on planet earth, has some personal level of time consciousness. It might not be as profound as our human sense of time, or it may be more profound, but none the less, it exists. The leaves fall off the trees in the winter, they flower in the spring and summer time, specific fruits and vegetables grow according to the changing seasons and in line with our own biological needs. Animals hibernate in the winter. Birds migrate in the summer and winter. The sun rises and sets every single day, at times that fall in line with the seasons.

We cannot ignore time. The clock is ticking. Ever faster the sand torrents into the bottom of the hourglass and still we fool ourselves into believing that we have the earth for all infinity. We need to look to the future to change the present, to change the future, to see that if we continue these patterns of behaviour we will destroy the earth and we will destroy ourselves. Snap shots of our future can help us to change our lives in the now, for the better.

We should not be looking to the future for material or physical gain. Neither should we obsess about every tiny little detail of the future and pin all our hopes on the future being the only arena for our positive transformation, without taking action in the present. We need to take action now, in the present, but still look towards the future for our self-development and spiritual growth. We can plan what we will do tomorrow, or the day after, or the day after that. We can know that in a few months our spiritual growth will have rapidly expanded, because every single day we will have taken action to ensure that outcome.

There are guarantees about the future and if we are intuitive and insightful enough, we start to become aware of those guarantees. Enlightenment breeds such awareness.

You do not have to be a constant clock watcher and panic about where you will bc in five minutes, ten minutes, thirty minutes or one hour. If you sit just watching time, you will waste time with your own inaction. Be aware of the time, but not to the extent that it overwhelms you.

We all have certain deadlines to work towards, we all have to be somewhere at a particular time, we all have to pay our bills by a certain time and date. We have to acknowledge time and respect time, without being obsessed with time to such an extent that we drift from our personal and spiritual growth. Worrying does not make our problems vanish and time does not make our problems dissolve; only solving them does. To solve our problems, we need to use intuition. There is always a balance to be found with anything and the same can be said for time.

So, what about the now? What about being in the now? Being in the present moment is important. We need to be conscious of everything we do and see in life. If we dwell on the past all the time or if we aspire to the future without making changes in the present, then we delay our spiritual growth. We need the past to learn from our mistakes, to learn lessons so that we can move on.

If we live constantly in the past, we forget about what we should be doing in the present *and* in the future. If we live only in the future, we do not learn the lessons from our past *and* we forget about what we should be doing in the present.

Now is important. Life can be perceived a series of 'nows' or moments, but this does not mean that you can negate the past or fail to prepare for the future. The past shapes who we are in the present and then we in turn shape the future based on our past. These three periods of time co-exist in perfect unison. We cannot shirk any one in favour of the others, because they are all a part of our earthly existence and we need to learn and grow from all three.

In short, what can be deduced from much of the literature and philosophy on being in the now is, do not dwell on the past and do not look to the future so much that you ignore the present. It has taken many additional fruitless words to make this single point, in much of the work we have seen on this subject. I will endeavour to be fruitless no more by overstating a glaringly simple concept.

The following techniques are intended to help you cultivate your foresight. As you become more aware and intuitive, you may start to gain insights into your future and the future of the Universe as a whole. These will help you on your journey on earth and will benefit the journey of your soul. These insights will also help you to understand your past. With this knowledge and insight you will have a better comprehension of the timescale you are working upon.

We are all going to take leave of this earth. That is inevitable. As we become more enlightened we can come to get a better grasp on how long we have left. We can then know how much we have to do in that time. This does not mean that we will become totally fixated upon the time we have left, or that we will constantly fret over it. Instead, we will just do what we need to do and act as we should act, knowing that once our journeys are completed on this earth, time will then, not matter. Time should not control us to such an extent that we lose ourselves. We should follow time to such an extent that we find ourselves.

"Learn from yesterday, live for today, hope for tomorrow. The important thing is not to stop questioning."

Albert Einstein

Techniques

Finding Foresight

 Sit down comfortably, either in a chair, or on the floor; make sure your back is straight.

 Place your palms over your eyes. As you breathe in through your nose, visualise a white beam of light coming down from up above, as far as the eye can see and entering the top of your head.

 As you breathe out, push the beam of light, down your neck, along your shoulders and arms, out of your hands and into your eyes and the back of your head. Continue the above two processes for between five and fifteen minutes.

 Place the index finger of your left hand, in the middle of your forehead, between your eyebrows. Place your right hand over you navel.

 Keeping your hands in position, silently say to yourself, with meaning and purpose, seventeen times, "May my intuition guide me to have the foresight I need."

 Rotate the index finger of your left hand, three times, anti-clockwise, in the mid point between your eyebrows.

 Pat your navel three times with your right hand.

 Join your hands in prayer position, in front of your chest and bow to the Universe.

Practise this exercise at least three times a week.

Universal Awareness

❑ Lie down comfortably, either on a sofa, the floor or on your bed. Place your palms, at the top of your chest, on either side.

❑ Breathe in slowly and deeply through your nose, visualising, the whole room engulfed in gold light. As you breathe out, through your nose, visualise that light being absorbed into your body, from head to toe. Continue this process for between three and fifteen minutes.

❑ Breathing normally and retaining the visualisation of the room and your body engulfed in gold light, imagine your spiritual body or soul, as a more luminous version of yourself, stretching and growing, until it reaches outside of your body. See your spiritual body grow taller, until it extends for miles and miles. Watch what is happening around you as your spiritual body stretches. Allow your spiritual body to take in the world, as you grow past it.

❑ When you feel your spiritual body can reach no further, maintain the visualisation of your spiritual body stretched, engulfed in the gold light and seeing everything from a much bigger perspective. Continue this process for between five and twenty minutes.

❑ Silently say to yourself, with meaning and purpose, "May my connection with my spiritual body grow stronger and may my awareness of the Universe increase as I need it."

❑ Give silent thanks to the Universe for all you have learned and continue to learn.

Conclusion

"The strongest principle of growth lies in the human choice."

George Eliot

We all have choices to make in life. We are blessed by our ability to choose and yet we are cursed by our reluctance to make judicious choices. This is the greatest barrier to our personal development and to our spiritual growth. Ignorance is so terribly easy to plead, but if we choose ignorance over enlightenment we have failed ourselves so miserably.

The arrogance of humankind over many centuries has distanced a great many of the earth's inhabitants from their souls, from compassion, from love, from the Light. As a species, we have grown so far away from the truth that we have become accustomed to living in the dark. It comforts and cossets us and promises our reward, but it punishes and feeds off us and we are too blind to see its cause. We feed our flesh instead of nourishing our souls. We live in the flesh but we are dead. For those who are brave enough to break free there is sanctuary. Find yours.

There are a great many obstacles to enlightenment, not to deceive us or trip us up, but because we meticulously crafted them, with each backward step. Time has moved us forwards but much of humankind has devolved backwards.

One of these barriers is a lack of compassion for all living things and a failure to learn from the teachings of time.

One fundamental, inherent intuition we have is to cherish all living, sentient beings. Jesus Christ condemned the ill treatment of any living being, as have numerous great and seminal thinkers, philosophers, religious leaders, scientists and physicians throughout the history of this earth. Russian novelist Leo Tolstoy, put it so well in his article, The First Step, when he said "This is dreadful...that man suppresses in himself, unnecessarily, the highest spiritual capacity – that of sympathy and pity towards living creatures like himself – and by violating his own feelings becomes cruel."

We kill by dining on the flesh of other beings that are of no less value than our own. History should have taught us otherwise, but we have failed to learn. If you can kill a living creature or acquiesce to its slaughter, you have dimmed the beautiful Light inside of you and darkened a part of your soul, where there should be only Light. How can one be enlightened if one is privy to butchery? The answer is one cannot. History has taught us how to amass better tools for our slaughter of all living beings. Though, despite this, there is still time for it to teach some of us, something.

This is merely one example, but there are many, many more. As we become more spiritually evolved, we have the ability to transcend these barriers and make the right choices for the right reasons, because we profoundly believe in them, not because we have been told of them.

That is the key to the paths that we lead, making choices through choice and not through the desire to please. We have to know deep inside, from the essence of our souls and then allow our thoughts and our actions to follow. If we act for the wrong reasons, we act without the awareness to match the intent. Our endeavours will be disingenuous and we will fall at the first hurdle. If our endeavours are born from the conflation with our souls, we will act with sincerity and integrity and eventually we will become whole.

Our words are utterly meaningless without physical actions to legitimise those words. As Eleanor Roosevelt so wonderfully put it, "One's philosophy is not best expressed in words; it is expressed in the choices one makes...and the choices we make are ultimately our responsibility." They are *our* responsibility because we have a choice. We can choose how we think and how we behave. We can choose to be conscious, every minute, of every hour of every day. We can live by our words and illuminate our paths to the Light, so that every step we take is not shrouded in darkness, but furnished with unconditional love and veracious insight. This choice is so infinitely precious and so unequivocally exquisite, if we would just all dare to make it.

And so, you can only achieve what is possible. Our mission is not one of attracting our own mortal desires; it is one of spiritual evolution and finding our way to the Light. We can achieve many things that we never believed possible, but the will of the Universe will always intervene. If we want what is not ours, our desires will not transpire, if they do, through our endurance, we must accept the consequences with humility.

Nothing is without a price and the price we must accept, or else, we heighten our own suffering and become burdened with our regret. We are fools among fools if we sincerely believe that we can accomplish whatever we desire, without an ounce of responsibility. We are wise men among fools if we take the time to truly see. Our mortal eyes can blur our vision, from our own reality.

You can fly, if you choose, to achieve the perfect dream of oneness with your soul that knows no division. Then your dreams will fall in line with the Universe's perfect vision. If you hanker after worldly wealth and satisfaction, you will be rich in earthly gains but you will be deprived of your soul connection. Then Poverty will be your name and you will know no resurrection.

Without the guidance of our souls, we are left out in the cold. The world is a dark and lonely place. If our souls guide our existence we are richer than all the gold, we have love, compassion and genuine happiness. Our foundations are strong and they branch out into the heavens, we have wisdom and peace of mind that will stay with us forever.

Although I penned this book with an air of high-spiritedness, throughout, the message is terribly serious and in truth, it is only this:

Find Your Way

Find Your Way

We are lead to believe that we can acquire our flesh desires
But we burn in the flames and we dance in the fire
We forget to beget light, to transcend our mortal souls
We take refuge in the pyre as we incinerate ourselves whole

The fire of compassion is diminished to a flicker
We would burn it out completely, would it go any quicker
We are drunk, we are lost, we are burdened by the shame
But is for the Devil's sport, for our torture is a game

Hear the cries, hear the screams, hear our souls begging please
Though it calls us, we ignore it; we are dragging on our knees
Wait a moment, stop and listen as the whisper starts to glisten
Turn the flicker to a flame; love the Light, there lays your mission

It is immortal, it is treasure, knows no bounds in all its glory
It is love, it is all; it is a never ending story
It awaits us as we step and we step in each direction
It is watching so intently, every footprint and inflection

Let it beckon, if you will, imbibe each drop of inner beauty
You are more precious than you know and your path is your duty
A precious Life in all perfection that knows no limitation
Can be yours, in Enlightenment, a cherished invitation.

Dawn Mellowship

About The Author

Dawn Mellowship is a Reiki practitioner and teacher. As well as treating a wide range of clients, she has taught Reiki to hundreds of students; helping them to transform their lives and use Reiki for the benefit of themselves and others. Dawn devotes her life to her own personal spiritual growth and promoting health and well-being to as many people as she can. Her Reiki work has been featured in a variety of publications including: Health and Fitness, Positive Health, Natural Health and Beauty and TNT and on Myspirit Radio station. Dawn is also a journalist and as Features Editor of a health and lifestyle magazine called Tonic, she regularly contributed articles about poignant issues and living a healthy, happy lifestyle.

B O O K S

SOME RECENT O BOOKS

Passage to Freedom
A Path to Enlightenment
Dawn Mellowship

"Passage to Freedom" is an inspiring title that combines a spiritual treasure trove of wisdom with practical exercises accessible to all of us for use in our daily lives. Illustrated throughout with clear instructions, the information and inspiration emanating from Dawn Mellowship is a major achievement and will certainly help all readers gain insight into the way through and around life's problems, worries, and our own emotional, spiritual and physical difficulties. **Sandra Goodman PhD**, Editor and Director, *Positive Health*

9781846940781 272pp **£9.99 $22.95**

The Essence of Reiki
The definitive guide to Usui Reiki
Dawn Mellowship and Andy Chrysostomou

Dawn and Andy are the first Reiki Masters in recent times to put forth the effort of restoring Reiki, a spiritual healing system promoting health and well being, towards the original goals and ideals of its founder Sensei Mikao Usui. This body of work inspires a new sense of spirituality that is currently deficient in the modern day worldwide Reiki community. Read this book to gain a deeper understanding of your Reiki practice, or let it inspire you to begin a new journey towards an incredible path of healing and self discovery for lifetimes to come. **Stephen Buck**, Certified Massage Therapist, Reiki Master Teacher

9781846940996 240pp **£11.99 $24.95**

Shamanic Reiki
Expanded Ways of Workling with Universal Life Force Energy
Llyn Roberts and Robert Levy

The alchemy of shamanism and Reiki is nothing less than pure gold in the hands of Llyn Roberts and Robert Levy. Shamanic Reiki brings the concept of energy healing to a whole new level. More than a how-to-book, it speaks to the health of the human spirit, a journey we must all complete. **Brian Luke Seaward,** Ph.D., author of *Stand Like Mountain, Flow Like Water, Quiet Mind, Fearless Heart*

9781846940378 208pp **£9.99 $19.95**

7 Aha's of Highly Enlightened Souls
Mike George

A very profound, self empowering book. Each page bursting with wisdom and insight. One you will need to read and reread over and over again! **Paradigm Shift**

1903816319 128pp **£5.99 $11.95**

A Call to Remember
Follow Your Heart, Change the World
Carol Lynn Fitzpatrick

Carol Fitzpatrick is at the cutting edge of human consciousness evolution. She offers clear, positive, and useful information and insights of practical relevance both for individual development and societal

change. Her work is also unique among metaphysical texts, providing a distinct shift from channeled work of recent decades. It will find a wide audience. **Mary Jane Banks**, Editor, Washington, DC
978-1-84694-140-5 352pp £11.99 $22.95

A Woman's Way
The transformative journey from hurt to happiness
Dena Michelli

Trust me; this book could save your life. From the moment I read the first line 'I come from a family of wounded women' I was hooked. Gentle, wise and compassionate, Dena takes you by the hand and takes you on a journey that will change you forever. **Erin Pizzey**, International author, poet and playwright

9781846940873 224pp **£11.99 $24.95**

An Exchange of Love
Madeleine Walker

A lovely book with a gentle and profound message about how closely our animal companions are linked to our triumphs and traumas, and an astonishing insight into how willing they are to be a surrogate for our stress symptoms and how instrumental they can be in our healing. Madeleine Walker is one of the best animal intuitives in the world. **Kindred Spirit**

978-1-84694-139-9 240pp **£9.99 $19.95**

Christy's Journey
Through 12 Past Lives
Peter Watson Jenkins

Christy's Journey introduces readers to reincarnation through the real life story of Christy, who under hypnosis discovers twelve past lives, both male and female, from ancient Rome to Britain, France, Italy, Africa, and America, spending time between lives on the Other Side. regression sessions with the author.

These stories are vividly described. The author's reflections take Christy's experience to a deep level of understanding, suggestive of reincarnation.

9781846940828 176pp **£9.99 $19.95**

Deep Equality
Living in the Flow of Natural Rhythms
Jocelyn Chaplin

For many years, Jocelyn Chaplin has worked at the cutting edge of therapy, politics and conscious living. In this book she pulls together all the marvelous ideas and intuitions we have been hearing and experiencing at conferences and workshops. This is a text that academics, activists and anyone involved with the future of humanity should read, allowing themselves to become inspired by what Chaplin means when she writes of Deep Equality. **Andrew Samuels**, Professor of Analytical Psychology, University of Essex

9781846940965 160pp **£9.99 $22.95**

Finding Heaven Here
John C. Robinson

Finding out that this world is Heaven is crucial for human survival. Otherwise in the frenzy of dissociation, our shadow games will annihilate the planet. John Robinson's passionate and finely researched book will inspire seekers to open their enlightened eyes and see the world as it is, and start working in Sacred Activism to preserve it.
Andrew Harvey, Author of *Son of Man*, *The Direct Path*, and *The Essential Mystics.*

978-1-84694-156-6 208pp **£9.99 $19.95**

From the Bottom of the Pond
The forgotten art of experiencing God in the depths of the present moment
Simon Small

Don't just pick this book up, read it and read it again. It's the best Christian book I have read in years. This is a book that will inform, delight, and teach. It needs to be heard. It has the potential to light up Christianity. This is what happens when God is happening. It's a brave book, expressing what it feels like to feel God. It shines a light on God in the midst of life, in the detail and the dirt, and it should be on every Christian's reading list. **Revd Peter Owen-Jones**, Anglican Priest, author and BBC TV presenter of *The Lost Gospels* and *The Battle for Britain's Soul.*

978-1-84694-0 96pp **£7.99 $16.95**

Gospel of Falling Down
The beauty of failure, in an age of success
Mark Townsend

It's amazing just how far I was drawn into Mark's words. This wasn't just a book but an experience. I never realized that failure could be a creative process. Editor, *Voila* Magazine

1846940095 144pp £9.99 $16.95

Graces for Today
Susan Skinner

A Grace book, or Book of Blessings, recognizes the free and open gift of God's grace. This small book however reaches out not only to believers, but to all people who may not define themselves as religious, yet who are open to the spirit and to the power of words.

9781846941283 64pp **£3.99 $5.99**

How to Be Happy
Finding a Future in Your Past
Jenny Smedley

The book provides proof that the work we do as past life therapists really does make a positive difference to peoples lives. A truly inspirational study of human behaviour. **Andrew Hillsdon**, Chairman of The Past Life Therapists Association

978-1-84694-150-4 196pp **£11.99 $24.95**

How to Meet Yourself
...and find true happiness
Dennis Waite

An insightful overview of the great questions of life itself: a compelling inner tapestry that encourages the reader to willingly embrace life being exactly as it is. Readable, relevant and recommended. **Chuck Hillig,** author of *Enlightenment for Beginners*

1846940419 360pp **£11.99 $24.95**

How to Read Your Horoscope in 5 Easy Steps
Chrissie Blaze

Chrissie Blaze has written THE book for anyone interested in learning astrology, and she's done it in a lively and witty style. Reading this is like having your own personal astrology teacher close at hand. It's aimed at beginner astrologers but also offers insights and revelations for experienced astrologers. It's a must have in everyone's metaphysical library. **Dr. John Holder,** Chairman, Festivals for Mind-Body-Spirit, U.K.

9781846940729 160pp **£9.99 $16.95**

I'm Still With You
True Stories of Healing Grief Through Spirit Communication
Carole J. Obley

Carole Obley's extremely well-written journey into mediumship is an inspiration to anyone wanting to understand life after death, connect with loved ones or with their own spiritual guidance. This must-read book makes mediumship understandable for anyone in an easy-to-read

format that transforms mysteries about life after death into realities.
Nancy Mramor, author of *Spiritual Fitness*

9781846941078 256pp **£11.99 $22.95**

Living With Honour
A Pagan Ethics
Emma Restall Orr

This is an excellent pioneering work, erudite, courageous and imaginative, that provides a new kind of ethics, linked to a newly appeared complex of religions, which are founded on some very old human truths.
Professor Ronald Hutton, world expert on paganism and author of *The Triumph of the Moon*

9781846940941 368pp **£11.99 $24.95**

Medicine Dance
One woman's healing journey into the world of Native...
Marsha Scarbrough

Beautifully told, breathtakingly honest, clear as a diamond and potentially transformative. **Marian Van Eyk McCain**, author of *Transformation Through Menopause*

9781846940484 208pp **£9.99 $16.95**

Mercury Retrograde
Your Survival Guide to Astrology's Most Precarious Time of Year
Chrissie Blaze

This exceptional treatment of how retrograde or stalled planets can stall your life offers yet more extraordinary proof that human beings are part of a giant energetic field of being. As one of astrology's brightest new stars Chrissie Blaze provides up much brilliant advice about how to navigate through life on hold. **Lynne McTaggart**, author of the bestselling *The Field*

9781846940736 240pp **£9.99 $19.95**

More Adventures in Eternity
From Henry to Higher Self
Gordon Phinn

A great contribution to the advancement of human Consciousness. It's a treasure trove of afterlife knowledge packaged in a marvellous series of firsthand retrieval and exploration accounts of his, and of some of the many non-physical Helpers and Guides of his acquaintance. Such a rich level of close-up details within these accounts gives readers much deeper insight and understanding into our existence beyond physical reality, and into the activities of our afterlife's inhabitants. In reading this fascinating and entertaining book readers will come to more clearly understand from a "big-C" Consciousness perspective who and what we human beings truly are. **Bruce Moen**, author of *Afterlife Knowledge Guidebook*

9781846940811 320pp **£11.99 $22.95**

Ordinary Secrets
Notes for your spiritual journey
Robert Y. Southard

Turned off by lofty teachers, levitating gurus, and approaches to spirituality that require years of training? Want to start today to live a more productive, relaxed, ecstatic life? If so, this is your book. In it Bob Southard shares his ordinary secrets that will send you on your way to an extraordinary life. **John Perkins**, *New York Times* Best Selling author of *Confessions of An Economic Hit Man*

9781846940675 96pp **£7.99 $16.95**

Ordinary Women, Extraordinary Wisdom
The Feminine Face of Awakening
Rita Marie Robinson

This will become a milestone in female spirituality. Not only does it recount the fascinating and intimate stories of twelve 'ordinary' women in their search for peace and self knowledge, the author engages the reader with her own quest through her integrity, vulnerability and courage. Beautifully written with captivating honesty, this unique book will become an inspiration for both men and women alike, also looking for the essence of who they truly are. **Paula Marvelly**, author of *Teachers of One*

9781846940682 256pp **£11.99 $24.95**